THE MIDDLE AGES

Jon Nichol and David Downton

CONTENTS

Basil Blackwell · Oxford

INTRODUCTION

The Middle Ages provides an outline course in British history from about 1150 to 1500 AD. Pages 1 – 40 examine the main topics in rough date order. Pages 42 – 61 study social topics. The contents of *The Middle Ages* add to those of *The Normans*. Together the two books give an extensive coverage of the period between about 1050 and 1500 AD.

The Middle Ages emphasizes the handling of historical EVIDENCE. It encourages the reader to think actively about the clues the past has left behind. On the basis of the evidence, he can form his own ideas about people and events, so building up a mental picture of the medieval world.

The book is carefully arranged for class, group or individual work. Each topic is self-contained and can be used for projects. The questions are roughly graded for difficulty, and give scope for pupils who work at different speeds.

Historians use clues or evidence to make up their minds about the past. On the front cover is a clue about an event in December 1170 AD. Look carefully at the picture. Then answer these questions.

a What is the man standing on the right holding in his hand? What kind of person is he?

b What do the four men standing on the left do for a living?

c Why has the kneeling figure joined his hands? What has happened to his hat? What does his hat tell us about his job?

d In what kind of building is the event happening?

e What is going on?

You can find out more about the event on the cover on pages 3-5.

EVIDENCE IN HISTORY
Edited by Jon Nichol

THE ROMANS   **THE MIDDLE AGES**
THE SAXONS   **THE TUDORS**
THE VIKINGS   **THE STUARTS**
THE NORMANS

ISBN 0 631 93390 5

Acknowledgements
Walters Art Gallery, cover, 47E, 56B; Mansell Collection, 4B, 23E, 36C, 50A; British Library, 5C, 12A, 34C, 42C, 45G, 54C; Courtauld Institute of Art, 10F; University Library, Cambridge, 11G; by gracious permission of H.M. the Queen, 14A; National Galleries of Scotland, 19E; WH0, 22A; C. James Webb, 22B; Mary Evans Picture Library, 24A, 30A, 31E; Camera Press, 24B, 29A; BBC Hulton Picture Library, 26A, 26B, 37D, 37E; Cambridge University Collection, 27E; Ghent University Library, 41F; Bodleian Library, Oxford, 47F; Crown Copyright, 48A; Newark Museum, 48E; Guildhall Library, 52B; Peter Newark's Historical Pictures, 55E.

© Jon Nichol 1981   Reprinted 1981

First published 1981
Basil Blackwell Publisher
108 Cowley Road
Oxford OX4 1JF
England

Printed and bound in Great Britain at The Pitman Press, Bath

MURDER IN THE CATHEDRAL: 29TH DECEMBER 1170

Commentator: Edward Grim, you were a monk living in Canterbury, Kent, (*see page 20, map* **A**) on 29th December 1170. You were with the Archbishop of Canterbury, Thomas Becket, when four knights arrived from the king, Henry II. Later, perhaps in 1175, you wrote about what happened. What did you say?

Edward Grim: The four knights forced their way into the hall. When Thomas heard they were there, he let them into a smaller room. For a long time nobody said a word. Finally Thomas spoke to them. The evil men, intent on murder, swore at him. They then said, "You are to blame that the king's bishops were thrown out of the Church. You have done wrong to expel so rashly the king's servants and priests from their Church posts. Take them back." Thomas answered, "How dare you threaten me. Be silent!" The knights became even angrier, and leapt to their feet. They pushed up close to him, and said, "Your words put you in danger of death." Becket said, "Your threats don't worry me. If you are ready to kill me, I am ready to die as a martyr." The knights left amid the curses and insults of the monks.

Commentator: Plan **A** helps you see where this happened. Clearly things were brewing up to a major crisis. Henry II's knights had gone out —perhaps they would go back to the king. Edward, what happened next?

Edward Grim: Soon these murderers came back. They wore all their armour, and carried swords and axes. They found the doors shut. So they chopped down a wooden barrier and got into the hall. The noise and chaos frightened most of the monks. They fled like sheep. Some monks begged Thomas to find safety in the cathedral. He refused. Then they dragged him into it.

After the monks had fled to the cathedral, taking Thomas with them, the four knights followed with quick steps. It was the time of the afternoon service. It stopped when the knights came in. The drawn swords, clanking armour

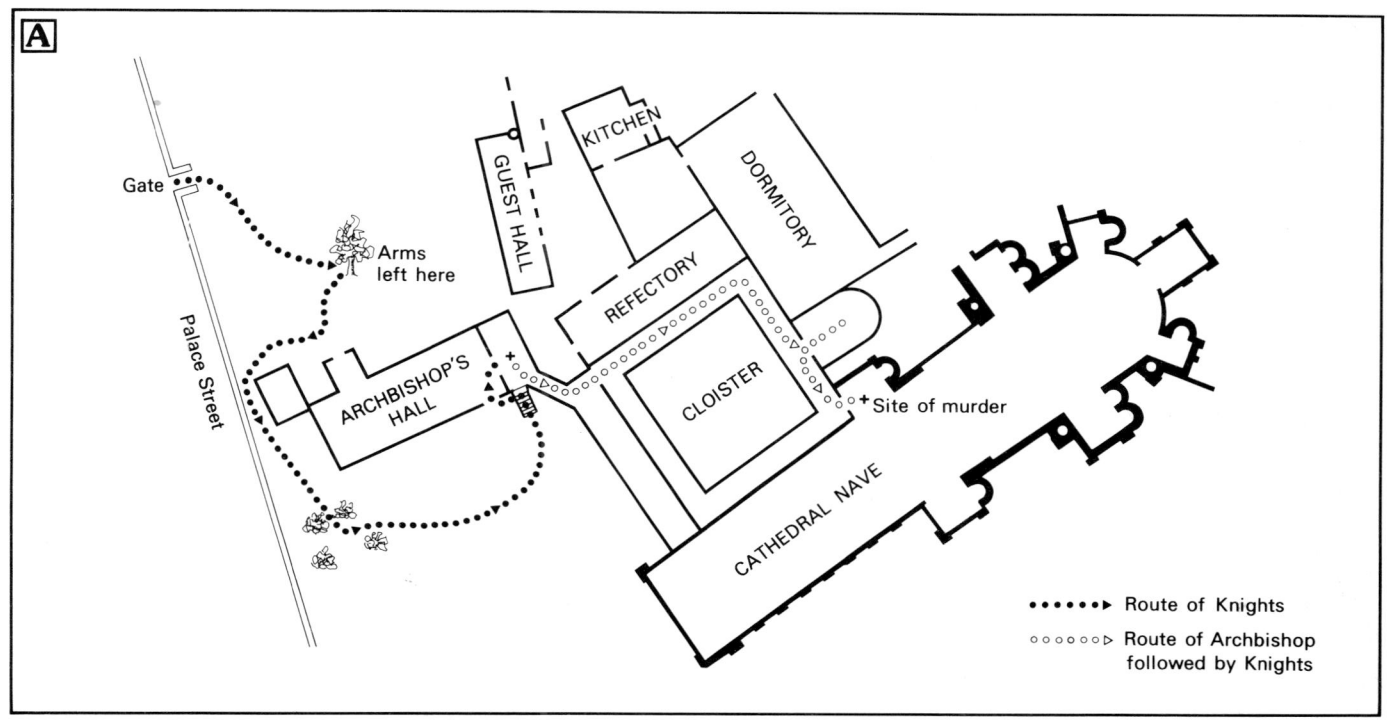

A

Gate

Arms left here

Palace Street

ARCHBISHOP'S HALL

GUEST HALL

KITCHEN

REFECTORY

DORMITORY

CLOISTER

+ Site of murder

CATHEDRAL NAVE

•••••• ▶ Route of Knights

○○○○○○ ▷ Route of Archbishop followed by Knights

and horrific looks of these wicked men terrified the monks. Mad with anger the knights shouted, "Where is Thomas Becket, traitor to king and country?"

Commentator: What did the knights do now?

Edward Grim: They shouted louder, "Where is the archbishop?" Without fear he replied, "I am here—a priest, not a traitor to the king. Say what you want from me." Their answer came, "Give back the Church posts of the men you have thrown out of the Church." "I will not," he cried. They bellowed, "Then die now, and get what's coming to you." He answered, "I am ready to die for my Lord." Then they rushed at him. Wickedly they tried to drag him out of the cathedral to kill him. But he grabbed hold of a pillar. So one of them gripped him more tightly. Fiercely Thomas shook him off, cursed him and shouted, "Don't touch me, Reginald Fitzurse. Have you all gone mad?" Thomas then bowed his head, and held up his hands together.

Commentator: The crisis point had been reach-ed. The archbishop was praying to God. Edward, how did the knight behave?

Edward Grim: The wicked knight feared that the people might rescue Thomas. Suddenly he leapt at Thomas and wounded him on the head. With the same blow that cut the top of his head he almost chopped off my arm. For I had remained with the saintly archbishop when everyone else had fled. I held my arms around him until I was wounded. A second blow hit his skull, but he still stood firm. With the third blow he fell on his knees and elbows. In a weak voice he said, "In Jesus' name and for the support of the Church I am ready to die."

As he lay there the third knight wounded him dreadfully. His sword sliced through his head and bit into the steps. The blow cut off the top of his head. Out spilled his white brains and red blood to stain the floor of the cathedral. The fourth knight kept back any who came near. A fifth man, a priest, had come in with the knights. He placed his foot on the neck of the holy martyr, and spread his blood and brains around the floor. He shouted out to the others, "Let's go, this chap won't get up again."

Commentator: **B** is a modern photograph of the scene of the murder. **C** a drawing of the events described above. **C** is from a medieval book. Thank you, Edward Grim, for this account of the murder of Archbishop Thomas Becket on 29th December 1170. For years he had been the closest friend of the king, Henry II. As Henry's chief minister or chancellor he had helped him run the country. In 1162 Henry had got Becket to become Archbishop of Canterbury. Becket was as good an archbishop as chancellor, when he had been ruthless in squeezing money out of the Church. As Archbishop, Becket changed completely. He refused to let the king run the Church for his own ends and milk it like a cow. They had bitter rows. Becket refused to let the king's men hold jobs in the Church—appointments which the head of the Church, the Pope in Rome, had to confirm. The row ended in tragedy on 29th December 1170.

C

1 What might it have been like to have been with the priest Edward Grim talked about in his last paragraph? As if you had been there, mention the following:

> riding with the knights to Canterbury; your talk; reaching Canterbury; enter the hall; talk to Becket; leave; go to cathedral; argument there; the fight with Becket; your part in Becket's death; you depart.

2 How reliable do you think is the evidence produced above about Becket's murder? Make out a table like the one below, with your comment after each question.

Evidence	Questions and Comment
Edward Grim's evidence, taken from his diary or chronicle of the events.	How reliable is it? COMMENT:
Cover picture	In what ways is it like Edward's account? Do you think it was drawn to illustrate Edward's story? COMMENT:
Picture **C**, page 5	In what ways is it like Edward's story? COMMENT:
Photograph **B**, page 4	What does it tell us about the murder? COMMENT:

3 Say what you think happened in Canterbury on 29th December 1170.

HENRY II: 1154-89

Four of Henry II's knights murdered Thomas Becket. What was Henry II like? Peter of Blois, a priest at Henry's court, wrote:

A *Our king is still red-faced, although old age and white hair have changed his colour a little. He is of average height, so that among small men he does not seem large, nor short among tall men. His head is a globe, as if the home of vast intelligence. The size of his head is matched to his neck and whole body. When he is peaceful his eyes are clear, lack cunning and seem dove-like. When in a rage they gleam like fire and flash like lightning. As to his hair, he is in no danger of going bald. However, his head is closely cut. He has a broad, square, lion-like face. His feet are arched, and he has the legs of a horseman. A broad chest and muscled arms show him to be a strong, brave, busy man. The roughness of his hands shows that he does not care about looks, for he never wears gloves except when hawking. . . . Although his legs are bruised and swollen from hard riding, he never sits down except on horseback or for meals. . . . He always has his weapons at hand when not busy talking or with his books. When business and worries give him breathing space, he spends time reading, or with a group of priests trying to solve a difficult question.*

Another priest, Gerald of Wales, wrote about Henry II just after he died.

C	**HENRY II'S GOVERNMENT**
Royal Taxes	Henry received money from his lands—*rents*; a special tax on people's moveable property—*tithe*; a fine when a person inherited land—*relief*; shield money from those unable to fight when called upon—*scutage*; money from the sale of *wardships*—heirs and heiresses under 21 in the King's care.
Royal Income: The Exchequer	A sheriff ran the King's affairs in each county. Each year the sheriff came to court to pay in the money he had collected for the King, and to account for what he had spent. The sheriff met the King's treasurer and other officials at the Exchequer table. This was covered with a cloth like a chessboard, to help work out the accounts.
Royal Spending	The King spent his money on the court; on expensive furs, clothes, silver and jewellery; on his castles, manor houses and hunting lodges; and on his army. The King could also pay his bills through grants of lands and privileges.
Royal Justice	The King and his chief judge, the Justiciar, tried important cases at court. The king's lesser judges travelled around the country to try minor cases, and to check that the sheriffs had justly enforced the law in their counties. The power of the King's courts was challenged by those of the Church. A church court's refusal to obey Henry caused the final quarrel with Becket.
Royal Army	Henry could order his chief barons to do military service—up to forty days a year. Often not enough soldiers came from this source for Henry's needs, and so he would hire others—*mercenaries*.
Local Government: The Sheriff	The sheriff carried out the King's orders in each county. Each county was divided into areas called hundreds. Each hundred had its own court. The sheriff was the judge for each hundred court, and tried cases from the villages.

B *Henry II, King of England, had a red, freckled face; a large, round head; grey eyes which glowed fiercely and grew bloodshot when angry; a fiery look and a harsh, cracked voice. His neck thrust somewhat forward from his shoulders, his chest was broad and square and his arms strong. . . . In times of war, which often threatened, he gave himself barely a second of peace to deal with other government business. In times of peace he did not allow a moment's rest. Beyond belief was his keenness for hunting. At the crack of dawn he was off on horseback, crossing heath, riding deep into forests and climbing mountains. So he passed restless days. On his return in the evening he was rarely seen to sit down before or after supper. His non-stop standing wore out his courtiers. He was very careful to protect and keep peace. In giving money to the poor he was generous beyond compare. Henry promised to defend the Holy Land. He loved the humble, condemned the proud and took care to keep the nobles in their place.*

How did Henry rule his lands in Britain and France—see **C**?

He travelled non-stop round his kingdom with his court. So he made sure that his great lords—his barons—obeyed him, that people paid his taxes and that he himself judged legal cases. Henry faced many problems. In particular the kings of France wanted his French lands. Later he had to face serious threats from his own family. His three sons, Richard, Geoffrey and John, rebelled against him. Their mother, Eleanour of Aquitaine, had left Henry, and encouraged her children to plot against him.

???????????????

1 **D** shows a medieval king like Henry II talking to some of his *council* of advisers—barons and bishops. The picture is of him and his bishops. What might it have been like to have been at a council meeting? Use **A** and **B** to describe Henry. Use these ideas to help you: his looks—height, face, body; voice; dress; hobbies and interests; behaviour to his council.

2 **C** shows how kings like Henry II ruled in the Middle Ages. Say how Henry:

   a raised money for a crusade;

   b dealt with a Scottish invasion if he heard news of it when he was in Gascony;

   c stopped the Pope from appointing bishops to English dioceses;

   d raised an army to fight the King of France;

   e handled the plotting of Eleanour of Aquitaine and their three sons.

3 Can we trust what Peter of Blois tells us about Henry II?

RICHARD THE LIONHEART: THE THIRD CRUSADE

Let us travel back in time to 1190. Richard the Lionheart, 1189-99, and the main rulers of Europe are getting ready to go on the Third Crusade to the Holy Land. Two years before, the Muslim leader Saladin had won back Jerusalem from the Christians. Now Europe intends to reconquer the city. Richard has agreed to lead the crusade with Philip Augustus, King of France. By June 1190 they are ready to set out. Richard is already a famous warrior. A writer of the time describes him.

. . . . He is tall, well built, with hair of a honey-yellow. His arms are rather long. This means that they are more useful than most men's for drawing and using a sword. His long graceful legs are straight, and match the rest of his body. He looks every inch a king.

How might you have fared as leader of a band of crusaders going with King Richard? **Crusader** will show you. It is a game for two people. To take part, all you need are a coin, your exercise book and something to write with.

CRUSADER

The winner is the player who reaches Jerusalem with most surviving knights. Each player has twenty in his band when he leaves France.

To Play
a Take turns in alphabetical order of your two surnames.
b On your turn, toss the coin to see what has happened to your band of men. You will either lose members, or new knights will join you. The numbers on map **B** tell you where you start each round. For example, Round 4 takes place in Cyprus.
c At the end of *each* round, make a full entry in your crusader diary. Use the information in table **C**, and anything else you can discover about the Third Crusade.
The quotes in this table are from a chronicle account of the Third Crusade, written by one of the crusaders, Geoffrey de Vinsauf.

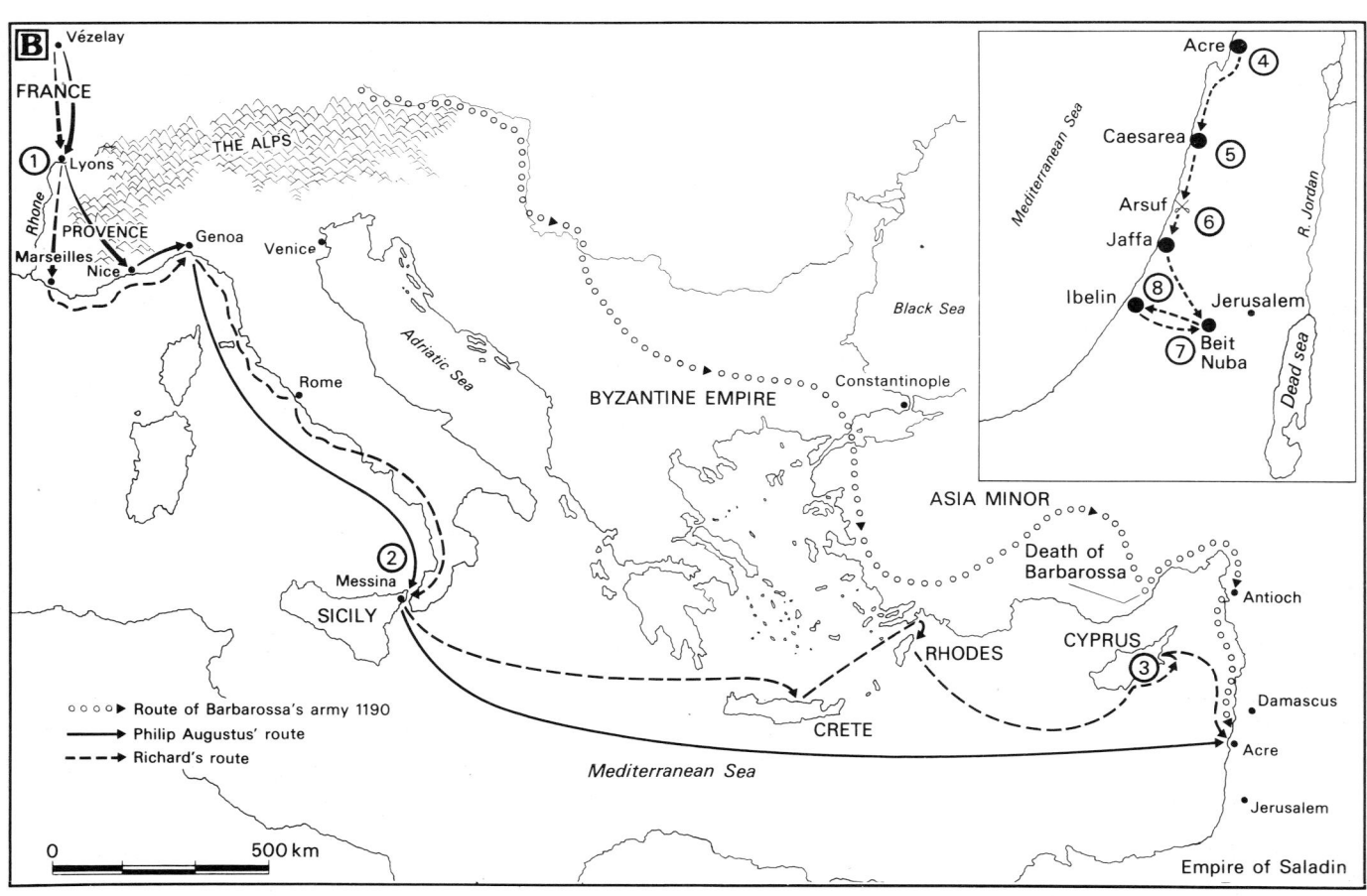

Key:
ooooo▶ Route of Barbarossa's army 1190
——▶ Philip Augustus' route
----▶ Richard's route

Round	Heads	Tails
1	Richard and Philip, King of France made a treaty to help each other, and to keep good faith with each other in every way. **(Gain 2 knights)**	*Richard came to the River Rhone, and ... gave way under his men's weight. As ... height, about a hundred men fell in.* **(Lose 3 knights)**
2	Richard sails from Marseilles to Messina in Sicily. Fighting breaks out in the city. *About ten thousand men marched in after him, and plundered the whole city. When our men entered the houses, the Sicilians threw themselves from the house tops, rather than fall into the hands of their enemies.* **(Gain 1 knight)**	*These wicked people . . . hostile to our men, annoy them by repeated insults and jabbing their fingers into their eyes and calling them stinking dogs, and mocking them in many other ways, privately killing some and throwing others into the sewers.* **(Lose 2 knights)**
3	Some of Richard's ships reach Cyprus, and are shipwrecked. *As to the sailors cast on shore, the Cypriots, pretending peace, greet and take them to a fort close by, and strip them of their arms.* **(Lose 2 knights)**	Richard's main fleet follows, and captures Cyprus after a fierce campaign. *The emperor fell on his knees in humiliation before Richard. . . . he would consider him Lord of everything else, if only he would not throw him into iron chains. . . . And the King bound the Emperor with silver, not iron chains.* **(Gain 1 knight)**
4	Richard sails from Sicily to Acre to meet King Philip of France. News arrives that the German emperor, Fredrick Barbarossa, has been drowned on his way to the Crusade.	
	The Turks threw Greek fire (a burning chemical) on Philip's catapults and other weapons of war, made with such care, and destroyed them. **(Lose 3 knights)**	*The chief men of the city went to the kings and offered to surrender, unconditionally, Acre, the Holy Cross and 250 noble Christian prisoners.* **(Gain 1 knight)**
5	The army marched from Acre towards Jerusalem.	
	The army had a very difficult march along the seashore on account of the great heat, and it was a long day's journey. Many of them, overcome by tiredness, dropped down dead, and were buried where they lay. **(Lose 1 knight)**	*The Saracens . . . suddenly attacked the pack-horses and loaded waggons, slew both horses and men in a moment, and plundered much of the baggage, boldly charging and scattering those who opposed them.* **(Lose 3 knights)**
6	Richard's army reaches Arsuf, where it fights a battle against Saladin's army.	
	The Turks, skilled bowmen, press their attack non-stop. It rained darts, the air was filled with showers of arrows, and the brightness of the sun was clouded by the huge number of missiles. **(Lose 4 knights)**	Richard leads a charge. *The enemy fled from his sword and gave way, while helmets tottered beneath it, and sparks flew from its strokes. So great was his fury, and so many and deadly his blows, that soon the enemy were all scattered.* **(Lose 1 knight)**
7	The Crusaders march towards Jerusalem, January 1192.	
	The army now rejoiced that they should soon set eyes on our Lord's tomb. All began to brighten up their armour, their helmets and swords, that there might not be a single spot to spoil their brightness. **(Gain 1 knight)**	Quarrels between the leaders of the Crusade cause Richard to retreat. *So great was the distress of the army that many abandoned their pilgrimage, cursing the day they were born to suffer such a disappointment. Some were so worn down by their sufferings and hunger that they could carry on only with difficulty. Their horses and baggage animals also, affected by the cold and rain, could not go on through the mud, but fell starved and crushed under their loads.* **(Lose 4 knights)**
8	Richard tries again to reach Jerusalem, but fails. He makes an agreement with Saladin *that peace should be strictly observed between Christians and Saracens, each free to come and go as they please. Pilgrims should have free access to the Holy Tomb without payment of any kind.* **(Gain 1 knight)**	*'O Jerusalem, now without help! Who will protect you, should the truce be broken, now that King Richard is leaving?'* Such were the words of each Christian, when the king set sail. **(Lose 1 knight)**

Richard spent most of the rest of his reign in France, fighting to win back castles and lands which the French King had conquered. In 1199, while riding near the walls of a town he was besieging, an arrow hit him in the shoulder, and a few days later Richard died. His brother John became King.

KING JOHN: 1199-1216

Do you know what happens if you are tried for a crime in court? Witnesses give evidence for or against you. Let us imagine that we are going to try a character from history—King John. Have you already heard of him? If so, note down what you know. We will look at some of the evidence against him. The **first accusation** against John concerns his quarrel with his nephew.

King John of England also ruled Normandy and Aquitaine in France; Arthur ruled Brittany. Arthur was the son of John's oldest brother. Arthur refused to obey John, and even claimed that he should be King. In 1202 John captured and imprisoned Arthur. Our first witness, a monk called Ralph of Coggeshall, says:

[A] *King John sent two men to Falaise to put out the eyes of Prince Arthur. Hubert de Burgh, the commander of the castle, refused. Filled with horror, he said that the orders were wicked and stupid.*

Arthur was moved to another castle. His new gaoler was William de Briouze. A monk from Margam in Wales tells us:

[B] *In the castle of Rouen, on the Thursday before Easter, King John was drunk after dinner, and under the influence of the devil. He slew Arthur with his own hand and tied a heavy stone to the body, which he slung into the River Seine. A fisherman caught it in his net. It was recognized and buried secretly, out of fear of the tyrant.*

Rumours told that John had Arthur castrated and blinded before his death.

Our **second accusation** against John is about his quarrel with the Pope. In 1206, John claimed that he should appoint bishops in England. Pope Innocent III said that he did not have this right. Did John mistreat nuns, monks and priests during their quarrel?

In 1208, John seized the church's lands, buildings and money. This was because the Pope had ordered priests to stop doing their normal jobs. They could only baptize babies and bless the dying. Our third witness, the monk Roger of Wendover, tells us:

[C] *The clergymen's corn was locked up, and sold for the King. The King's servants rounded up the priests' ladies, and they had to pay dearly to get them back. The King's men dragged from their horses priests of all kinds, and robbed and beat them. Afterwards the King's courts refused to help them. The servants of a certain sheriff on the Welsh borders brought to the King a robber they had caught. He had robbed and murdered a priest on the road. They asked the King what they should do with him. Straight away John replied, "He has slain an enemy of mine, release him."*

The quarrel between King John and the Pope dragged on until 1213, when they made a treaty.

The **third accusation** concerns John's quarrel with his barons: did he brutally ill-treat their families? In 1215-16 the main nobles of England rebelled against him. One was William de Briouze and his family. Our third witness, Roger of Wendover, claimed that King John:

D . . . . *made prisoners of them and sent them to England heavily chained. He ordered them to be carefully guarded in Windsor Castle . . . the noblewoman Matilda (William de Briouze's wife) died of starvation.*

The **fourth accusation** concerns the loss of the crown jewels, including the crown, in the Wash (see page 20, map **A**): Was John to blame, through lack of care? Again the main witness is Roger of Wendover.

E . . . *He passed through the town of Lynn. Its people received him with joy, and gave him large presents. Then he marched north. But, in crossing the river Wellester, he lost all his waggons and baggage horses, together with his money, priceless vessels and everything—men and horses. No one escaped to tell the King of the disaster. He himself narrowly escaped, with his army.*

King John lost the crown jewels while on campaign against the barons. In June 1215 they had forced him to grant them a charter of rights—Magna Carta. Pages 12–13 look at its terms. In September 1215 John refused to obey one of its main points—that a committee of twenty-five barons would enforce its terms. Civil war broke out again between King John and his nobles. After he lost the royal treasure in the Wash in October 1216, John reached Newark in Nottinghamshire (see page 20, map **A**). That night he feasted on rough cider and peaches, and fell very sick. A day later he died.

?????????????

1 In what ways are the people in **F** being tortured? What is happening to the two ladies in **G**?
or draw a strip cartoon to show how John treated his enemies.

2 Do you think King John was guilty of the charges against him? Make out a table like this one:

i Quarrel with his nephew: did he murder Arthur?
Nature of the evidence:
True or false:

ii Quarrel with the Pope: did he mistreat monks, nuns and priests?
Nature of the evidence:
True or false:

iii Quarrel with the barons: did he brutally illtreat their families?
Nature of the evidence:
True or false:

iv Loss of the crown jewels: was John responsible through gross negligence?
Nature of the evidence:
True or false:

MAGNA CARTA

Have you heard of Magna Carta—Latin for the Great Charter? Many of the rights we have today are based on it. What was Magna Carta about? When and why was it drawn up? To find out, we must travel back 750 years to a meadow on Runnymede Island (see page 20, map **A**) in the River Thames.

King John is sitting at a table with a list of barons' and bishops' demands in front of him—Magna Carta. The great charter is a peace treaty between him and his enemies. Their leader is Stephen Langton, Archbishop of Canterbury. The Pope has appointed him to make sure that King John keeps his promises when his quarrel ends. Many of the barons and bishops hate King John. They want to make sure that he can no longer seize their lands and money, or force them and their men to fight for him, or imprison them and their families.

Their chance to stop King John came in 1214. In October John returned to England from France. He had just lost the battle of Bouvines where the French King had smashed his army. It was the last and most disastrous of John's French campaigns. He had lost most of his lands in Normandy. He had forced the barons to pay for the war, and send soldiers. The great charter was aimed to stop him doing this. Talks between John and his enemies took place from January to June 1215. John tried hard to trick the lords, but failed. By June they had forced him to accept their terms.

Magna Carta is a long document—63 clauses—see **A**. It tells us about the quarrel between John and the lords, and why the great charter is the basis of our freedom today.

1 . . . *the English Church shall be free* (especially to choose its own bishops and have its own courts).

2 *If any earl, baron, or other person that holds lands* (fee) *directly of the Crown, for military service, shall die, and at his death his heir shall be of full age and owe a relief* (money to get his fee), *the heir shall have his inheritance* (lands) *on payment of the old scale of relief.*

5 *For so long as a guardian is in charge of an heir's land he shall use money from it to keep up the houses, parks, fish ponds, other ponds, mills and everything else belonging to it.*

6 *We* (The King) *may give heirs in marriage, but not to someone of a lower class.*

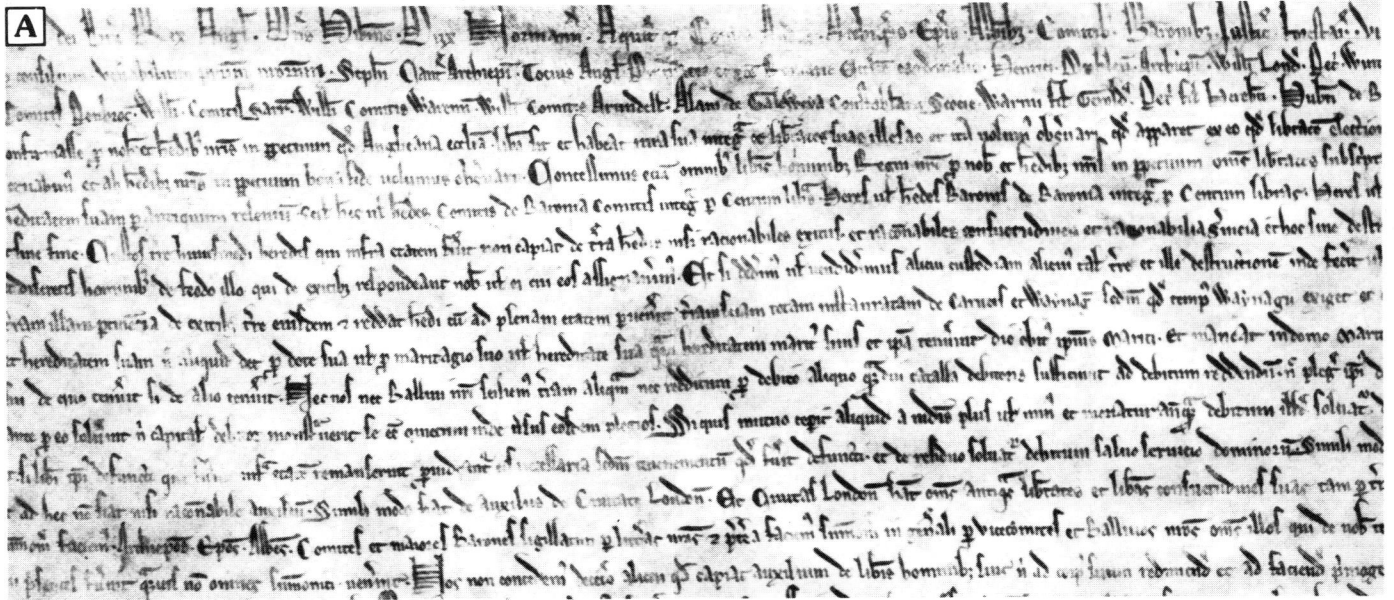

A

12 *No scutage (shield money) or aid (cash) may be raised in our kingdom without general consent, unless to ransom ourself, to make our eldest son a knight and, once, to marry our eldest daughter.*

13 *The City of London shall have all of its ancient freedoms and customs, both by land and by water. Likewise all other cities, boroughs, towns and ports . . .*

14 *To get the general consent of the Kingdom for the size of an aid. . . . or a scutage, we order the archbishops, bishops, abbots, earls and greater barons to be called by letters sent to each one.*

16 *No man shall be forced to perform more service for a knight's fee. . . . than is due from it.*

17 *Normal law courts shall not travel with the Royal courts, but shall be held in a fixed place.*

20 *For a minor offence a free man shall pay a fine that relates to the crime, and likewise for a major offence. The fine shall not be heavy enough to take away his livelihood.*

23 *No town or person shall be forced to build bridges over rivers except those who always had to do so.*

24 *No sheriff, constables . . . or other officials are to try cases that should only be tried by the Royal judges.*

30 *No sheriff, royal official or other person shall take horses or carts for transport from any free man, without his consent.*

33 *All fish weirs shall be removed from the Thames, the Medway, and throughout the whole of England, except the seaside.*

35 *There shall be standard measurements for wine, ale and corn. . . . There shall also be a standard width for dyed cloth.*

38 *In future no official shall put a man on trial upon his own evidence, without trustworthy witnesses to support him.*

39 *No free man shall be seized or imprisoned or stripped of his rights or possessions or outlawed or exiled, or deprived of his standing in any other way, nor will we use force against him, or send others to do so, except by the lawful judgement of his equals or by the law of the land.*

40 *We will neither sell, delay nor deny right or justice to anyone.*

41 *All merchants may enter or leave England unharmed and without fear, and may travel within it, by land or water, for purposes of trade, free from all illegal demands.*

45 *We will appoint as judges, constables sheriffs or other officials only men that know the laws of the kingdom and will keep them well.*

51 *As soon as peace returns, we will send from the kingdom all the foreign knights, bowmen, their men and mercenaries, who have come in, to its harm, with horses and arms.*

? ? ? ? ? ? ? ? ? ? ? ?

1 Do you have any serious worries about how you are treated? If so, set them out clause by clause in a charter like Magna Carta.

2 Make your own copy of the list **B** below: **a** = peasant, **b** = local merchant, **c** = baron, **d** = bishop. Read through each clause of the charter and put a ring round which person you think would benefit most from that clause.

B

Clause			Clause			Clause		
1	a b c d		2	a b c d		5	a b c d
6	a b c d		12	a b c d		13	a b c d
14	a b c d		16	a b c d		17	a b c d
20	a b c d		23	a b c d		24	a b c d
30	a b c d		33	a b c d		35	a b c d
38	a b c d		39	a b c d		40	a b c d
41	a b c d		45	a b c d		51	a b c d

3 Using the evidence of Magna Carta, say what life might have been like for peasants, barons, merchants and townspeople in the area where you live, first in 1212 and then in 1217.

4 How have clauses 38, 39 and 40 protected the freedom of all English people since 1215?

PARLIAMENT

Do you know who your local member of Parliament is, and how we choose him? He is a member of the House of Commons—one of the two Houses of Parliament. The other is the House of Lords. The head of Parliament is the Queen—Elizabeth II. She opens each session and signs all laws that Parliament makes. Parliament is also the highest court in the land. It has slowly won these powers over the last 700 years.

Parliament first met on the wishes of the King. The King wanted to talk—*parley*—with his leading subjects about his problems. The King was completely in charge of Parliament, and could send its members home if he did not like what they said. Picture **A** shows Parliament at the end of the Middle Ages. It gives us a clue about who went to it and how important they were.

Parliament grew out of the meetings of the King's *Great Council*. The King summoned his Great Council when he needed advice. Its members were his leading bishops and barons. Parliament began to win power in the reign of Henry III (1216-72), John's son and a weak king. In 1258, Henry III handed over power to a group of barons. Their leader was Simon de Montfort. To help him rule, he called regular meetings of the Great Council. In January 1265 he summoned a new kind of Great Council. As well as bishops and barons, he asked each county or shire to send two knights, and important towns to send two citizens or *burgesses*. Simon needed the knights and burgesses because many barons refused to back him. In the summer of 1265, Simon's enemies defeated and killed him at the Battle of Evesham.

Parliament usually met in halls of the Palace of Westminster, London. Picture **A** shows the hall where the Lords met. It also shows the members of the Commons attending this joint meeting. The Speaker is standing at the entrance. They had their own building—usually St. Stephen's chapel. The House of Commons has the same seating plan today.

The leader of the army against Simon was Henry III's son, Edward. As Edward I (1272-1307), he took up Simon de Montfort's idea of a bigger Great Council. Often he asked the knights and burgesses to its meetings. These parliaments would agree to the King's wish to raise taxes. In return the King would agree to their wish to pass laws. Parliament was also the King's most important court. **B** shows who went to Parliament. It took a long time for Parliament to take its modern form.

B

People in A	How Chosen	Their Powers
A The King	He usually inherited the crown from the last King as his oldest son.	As the country's ruler the King had the right to call a meeting of Parliament, and decide what business it did.
B The Archbishops of York and Canterbury	The Pope appointed the English Church's archbishops.	The archbishops were in charge of the English Church. Often they and other bishops worked as the King's ministers, helping to run the government.
C Bishops and Abbots	The Pope appointed them.	They were the leading members of the Church. The bishops were in charge of their dioceses, the abbots looked after their wealthy monasteries.
D Members of the House of Lords—*peers*: e.g. earls, barons	The King made them or their ancestors lords. The oldest son inherited the title on the death of his father.	Along with the other members of the House of Lords, they voted on laws, trials and taxes. Many peers were the King's ministers.
E The King's ministers	The King appointed them.	They were the most important members of government.
F Clerks	The King appointed them.	They recorded the business of the House of Lords.
G Members of the House of Commons	The King granted towns the right to elect one or two MPs called *burgesses*. He also allowed each county to choose two MPs— knights of the shire. Elections were held when the King called a new meeting of Parliament.	Members of the House of Commons voted on laws and taxes.
H The Speaker	The Members of the House of Commons chose him.	He was in charge of the business of the House.

? ?

1 Who and what would a person in **A** have seen inside Parliament? Mention all the government members described in **B** or draw a picture to show who they were.

2 If you look carefully at **A** you will see that the figures are all different sizes. Their sizes give an idea of how important they were. Put these figures in order of importance: the Commons, the Archbishops, the Peers, the King.

3 To show how Parliament changed in the Middle Ages, write a sentence on each of these: the Great Council; Simon de Montfort; Edward I.

4 Find out as much as you can about our modern Parliament, and say how it has changed since the Middle Ages.

EDWARD I AND WALES

Edward I, (1272-1307) was a first class soldier and general, and wanted to be a strong ruler. In Wales he faced a major problem in 1277. The ruler of Wales, Prince Llewellyn, refused to obey him. Llewellyn had built up his own kingdom in North Wales. He forced minor Welsh chiefs to obey him, and captured many of the border lands of Edward I's English barons. Edward I decided to attack and conquer Wales. **A** lists his possible plans of campaign.

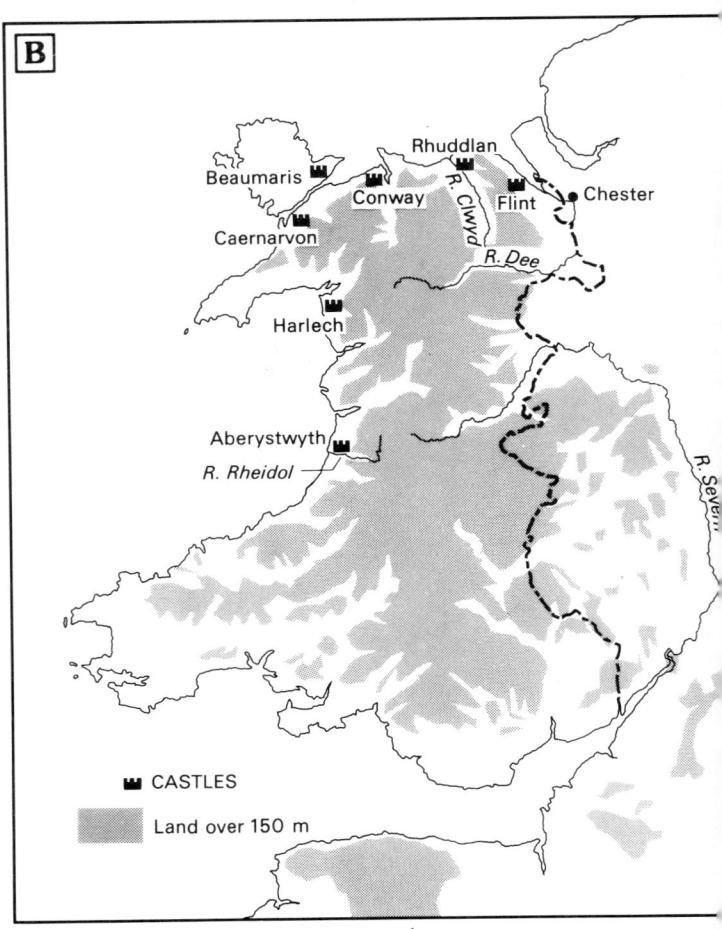

B

CASTLES

Land over 150 m

Beaumaris, Rhuddlan, Conway, R. Clwyd, Flint, Chester, Caernarvon, R. Dee, Harlech, Aberystwyth, R. Rheidol, R. Severn

A

a Invade Wales *either* with a single army which would march through Wales, destroying and killing wherever it went.

Or with three small armies, one to attack North Wales, one central Wales, and one South Wales. Ships would supply the northern army from Chester.

b Ally with Welsh leaders who dislike Llewellyn. These include the princes of South Wales and Llewellyn's brother, David.

c Build castles at key points to control Welsh lands. Map **B** shows the possible sites for the castles, and trading towns that would grow up by them. At any one time Edward could put up castles at:

either Flint and Rhuddlan on the north coast. These control important valleys.

or Conway and Caernarvon. These cut off Anglesey from the mainland. Anglesey was Llewellyn's major source of food and soldiers.

or Beaumaris. This keeps Anglesey from rebelling.

or Aberystwyth and Harlech. These keep down rebellion in Llewellyn's southern lands.

d Let the Welsh keep their language and ways of life. Edward could also offer to have his eldest son brought up as a Welshman, to be Prince of Wales.

??????????????

1 Look at list **A** and map **B**. What problems would a band of English knights have in fighting Llewellyn's men in central Wales in 1277? Llewellyn's men wore little armour, used short powerful bows, and liked to ambush their enemies. They could move quickly on foot or horseback.

2 Draw up your own plans for conquering and subduing the Welsh in 1277. Put plans **a-d** in list **A** into the order in which you would carry them out. Give your reasons for choosing each plan and how you hope it will work out. For **A** say which plan of campaign you would adopt. For **B** put the castles in the order in which you would build them. In time Edward built castles at all these places.

CONCENTRIC CASTLE

Edward I campaigned against the Welsh three times—in 1277, 1282 and 1294-95. In 1277 he defeated Llewellyn, who promised to obey him. Llewellyn kept most of his lands, but rose again in 1282. Llewellyn's forces were crushed, and he died in the fighting. His kingdom fell under English rule, and was split up into counties. In 1294-95 Edward smashed a final Welsh rising, and by 1296 he had carried out all the plans in list **A**.

Edward's castles were *concentric*—with two or more rings of defence. Each ring was made up of walls and towers. If an attacker captured the outer ring, he would still face an inner ring of higher walls and towers. The castle would not surrender until all the towers had been captured.

C shows the site of one of Edward I's concentric castles in Wales. Master James of St. George, a famous castle-builder, planned it. If you were advising Master James, how would you design a castle for this site? Consider points **a**—**h**.

a The castle walls must link up with the town walls.

b You can afford to build a castle with: 4 main towers and 24 small ones;
or 6 main towers and 16 small ones;
or 8 main towers and 8 small ones.

c Each tower in a ring of defence must be within *effective* bow range of the next tower—about 30 metres.

d The rings of walls and towers must be no more than 30 metres apart.

e A moat or dry ditch should be dug around the outer ring.

f The river must be straightened and deepened so that ships can carry supplies and men to the castle.

g A tower must be built on the river, with walls linking it to the outer ring of defence. Ships can unload in safety at the tower.

h Gateways can be made for both outer and inner rings of defences by putting two towers together.

By 1282 Master James had built a castle on site **C**—Rhuddlan, North Wales. Find out how well your castle compares with this one. Say what problems Welsh attackers would face in trying to capture your castle.

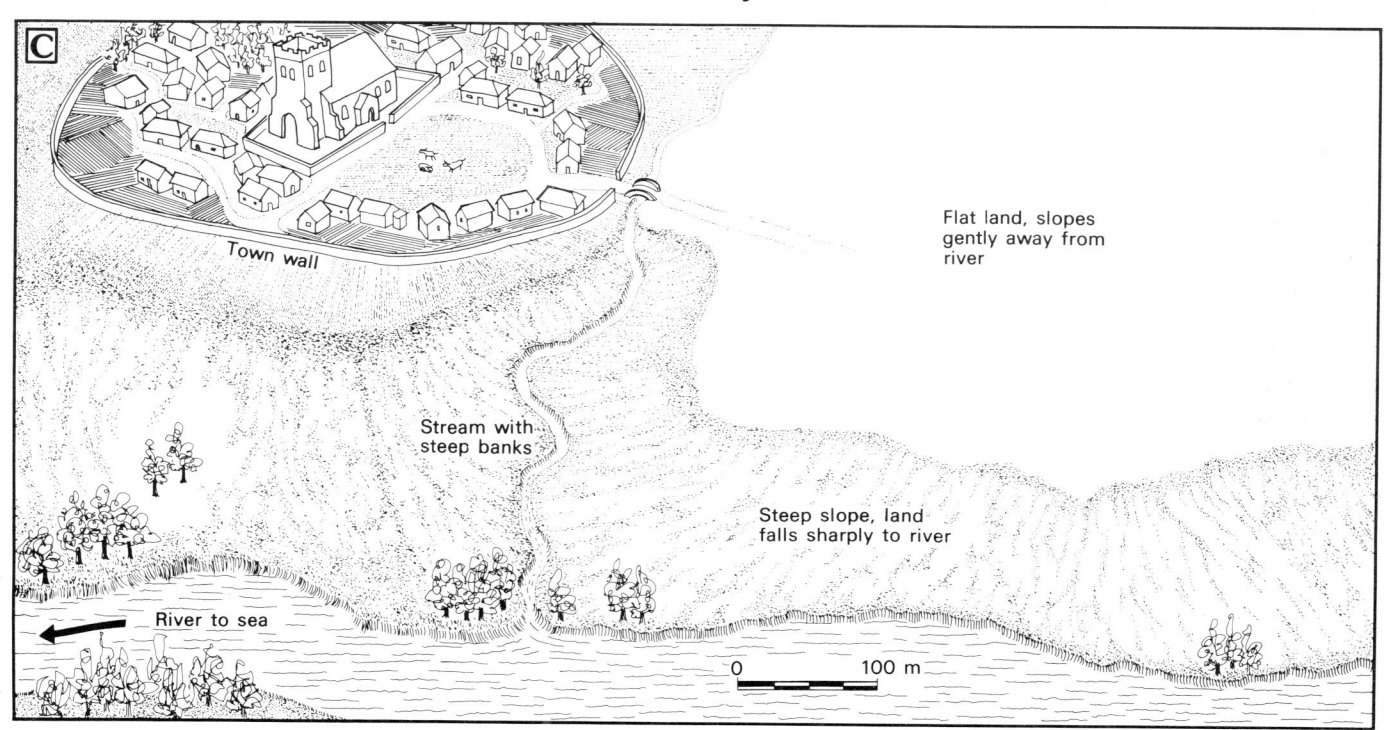

Town wall

Flat land, slopes gently away from river

Stream with steep banks

Steep slope, land falls sharply to river

River to sea

0   100 m

SCOTLAND AND THE BATTLE OF BANNOCKBURN

24th June 1314. Two armies faced one another at Bannockburn, Scotland (see page 20, map **A**). One was the English army commanded by King Edward II (1307-27): the other was the Scottish army commanded by Robert Bruce, see map **A**. The battle was to decide who would rule Scotland—Edward II or Robert Bruce. What had led up to the battle? Table **B** helps you see.

The English army at Bannockburn was about 17 000 strong. 2000 were knights, and 15 000 foot soldiers and archers, mainly longbowmen. The Scottish army was about 5000 strong. Five hundred were lightly armed knights, and the rest foot soldiers with long spears, or archers who used shorter and less powerful bows than the English. The Scottish foot soldiers fought in bands which, when massed together, looked from a distance like a hedgehog.

How did the battle go? On the evening of

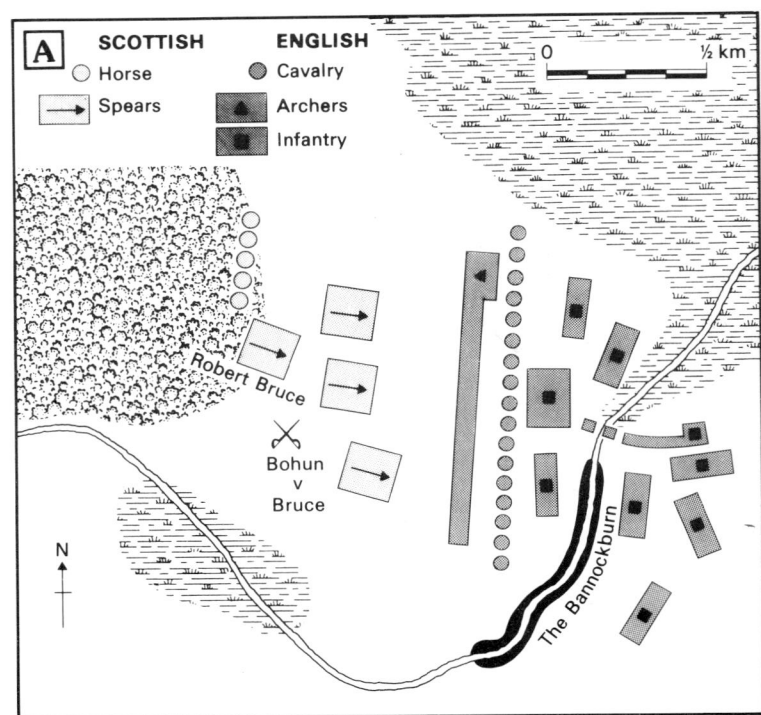

B
1292 John Balliol was crowned King of Scotland. His protector was Edward I, King of England.
1295 Twelve Scottish barons and bishops deposed John Balliol. They made an alliance with France. France was at war with England.
1296 Edward I conquered Scotland.
1297 The Scots rebelled against Edward I.
1305 The English captured and beheaded the Scottish leader, William Wallace.
1306-7 A new Scottish leader, Robert Bruce, emerged. Edward marched into Scotland, and Robert Bruce was forced into hiding.
1307 Edward I died. Edward II became King of England. Under Robert Bruce, the Scots fought back, and reconquered most of Scotland.
1314 June. Edward II invaded Scotland.

23rd June, Robert Bruce had killed an English knight, Henry de Bohun, in hand-to-hand combat. At dawn next day Bruce drew up his army in four massed bands of spearmen—*schiltrons*. One of these he kept in reserve.

Map **A** shows the two armies at the start of the battle. The English had their backs to Bannockburn, which ran through a gorge and then into a marsh. Many years later a writer got this account from an eyewitness.

C *When both sides were ready to fight, the English archers were put in front of the battle line (of knights). The Scottish archers fought with them, and on both sides a few were killed and wounded. But the King of England's archers soon put the others to flight. Now when the two armies had drawn close, all the Scots knelt to say the Lord's Prayer. After this they advanced boldly against the English. They arranged the army* *with two columns side by side in front of the third. In the third was Robert Bruce. We think in fact that there were three columns in the front line). Truthfully, when the armies clashed and the great horses of the English charged the pikes of the Scots as if into a dense forest, there arose a great and terrible sound of broken spears and fatally wounded war horses.*

So there was stalemate for a while. Now the English in the rear could not reach the Scots because the front line was in the way. Nor could they do anything to help themselves. Therefore there was nothing left but to flee.

This story I heard from a man I can trust, who was an eyewitness.

The English in the rear seem to have fled because:

D *In the front line were killed the Earl of Gloucester, Sir John Comyn, Sir Pagan de Typtoft, Sir Edmund de Mauley and many other nobles, besides foot soldiers who fell in great numbers. Another disaster that the English suffered was this. Shortly before, they had crossed a great ditch into which the tide flows. Now wanting to recross it, in the chaos many nobles and others fell into it with their horses, while others escaped with much difficulty. Many never got out of the ditch. Thus for many years the English spoke of Bannockburn.*

E is a later drawing of the battle.

Bannockburn meant the end of English rule in Scotland, which became an independent country under King Robert Bruce. In 1328 the new English King, Edward III (1327-77) made a treaty with the Scots which accepted their freedom.

Edward III was a strong ruler. But during his reign he had to face one problem he could not cope with—the Black Death.

E

???????????

1 Do you have a nickname? If so, how did you get it? On Edward I's tomb, in Latin, his nickname is written: *Here Is Edward The First, Hammer Of The Scots*. How did Edward get his nickname? Did he deserve it?

2 On your own map of the Battle of Bannockburn, mark the different stages of the battle. At the bottom of your map, list the points that helped the Scots to win.

3 What was it like at the Battle of Bannockburn? Imagine you were alongside the eyewitness from whom the writer of **C** and **D** got his account of the battle. Say what you saw, heard and smelt, and what your thoughts and feelings were. Use these ideas: early morning; talk of Bruce's victory yesterday; small number of Scots; battle lines drawn; archers; charge; chaos; screams; blood: swords; spears; panic; retreat.

4 How reliable are **C**, **D**, and **E** as evidence about the battle?

THE BLACK DEATH ARRIVES

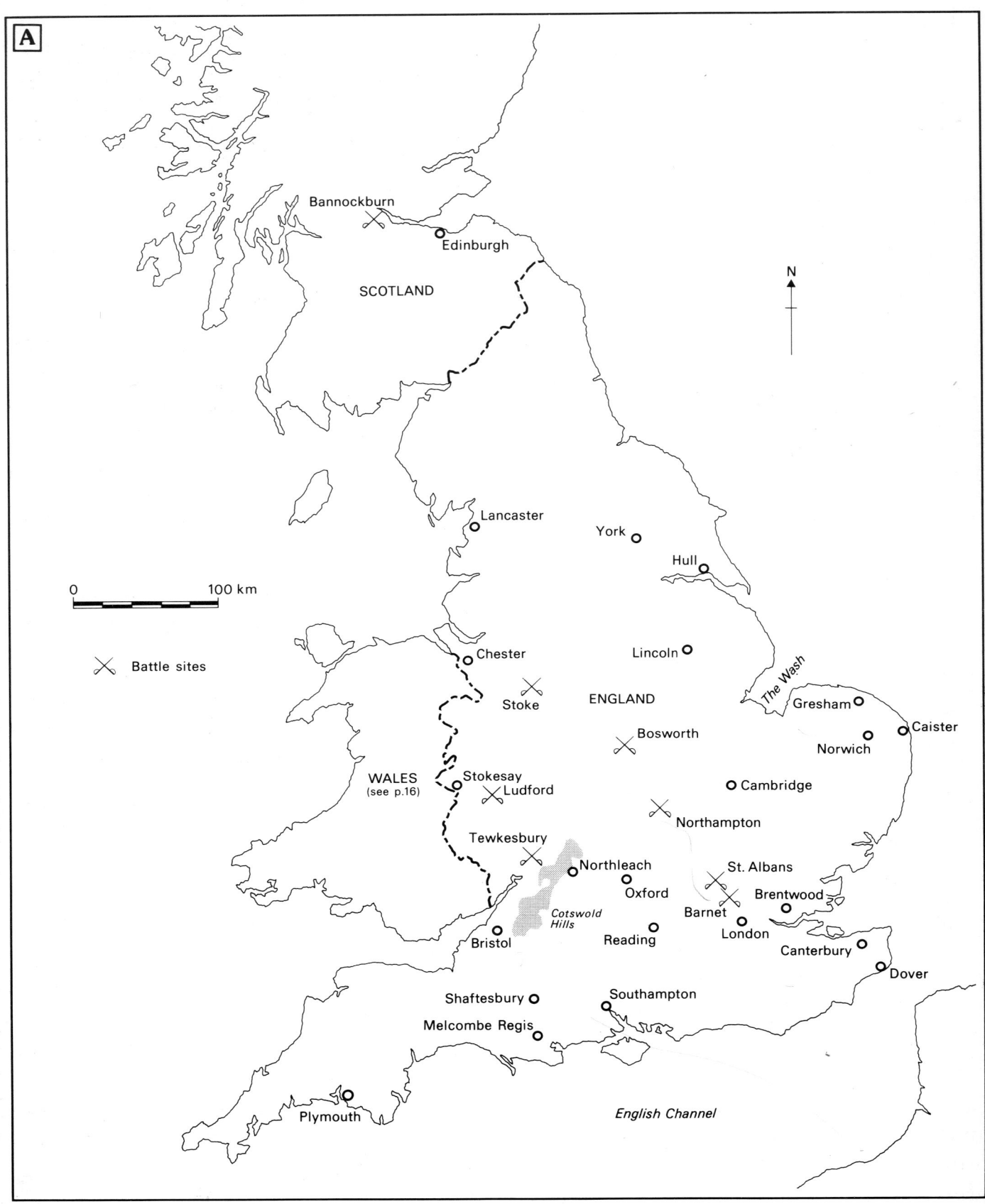

A

Bannockburn ✕

Edinburgh ○

SCOTLAND

N

0   100 km

✕ Battle sites

Lancaster ○

York ○

Hull ○

Chester ○

Lincoln ○

ENGLAND

The Wash

✕ Stoke

Gresham ○

Caister ○

Bosworth ✕

Norwich ○

WALES
(see p.16)

Stokesay ○
✕ Ludford

Cambridge ○

Northampton ✕

Tewkesbury ✕

Northleach ○

St. Albans

Cotswold
Hills

Oxford ○

✕ Barnet

Brentwood ○

Bristol ○

Reading ○

London ○

Canterbury ○

Dover ○

Shaftesbury ○

Southampton ○

Melcombe Regis ○

Plymouth ○

English Channel

Nursery rhymes often tell of important events in history. Sometimes they remind us of disasters. *Ring-a-ring o'roses* is one of these rhymes. Hundreds of years ago children danced to this rhyme during times of *plague*—a deadly disease. The rhyme tells what happened if you caught the plague. Some chroniclers, mainly monks, wrote about the plague that swept across England in 1348-49, map **A**. One such chronicle tells us:

B *In this year, 1348, in Melcombe Regis, in the county of Dorset, a little before the Feast of St. John the Baptist (24th June), two ships docked. One was from Bristol. From France one of the sailors brought with him the terrible plague. Through him the men of the town of Melcombe were the first in England to catch it.*

This plague is often called the *Black Death*. Fleas spread it from the black rat, **C**. It probably broke out in China several years before it reached Britain. Travellers brought it first to Russia, and then the rest of Europe.

Church records show that by the Autumn of 1348 the plague was common throughout Dorset. From there it moved west to Somerset and Devon, and north-east to London, where it was raging by November. The plague spread steadily northwards, and reached Norwich in January 1349. In Lincoln and Hull, four out of every ten priests died.

The plague was only one of many disasters that medieval people had to endure.

D *As for Hull, the King in 1353 let it off certain taxes . . . He considered the loss and destruction which our town of Kingston-upon-Hull has suffered, both through flooding of the Humber and other causes, and the death of a great part of the people in the last deadly disease which raged in these parts.*

A close look at church records in Dorset shows that the plague was at its peak in December and January. By February it was on the wane. At Shaftesbury, a town in North Dorset, new vicars had to be appointed in November and December 1348, and January and May 1349.

???????????????

1 The nursery rhyme ends "Atishoo, Atishoo, we all fall down!" What does this tell us about the Black Death?

2 Look at map **A**. Mark on your own outline map when you think the plague reached:
  a where you live;
  b Melcombe, London, Norwich, Hull, Scotland.

3 Imagine that a friend comes into the classroom to say a deadly disease has broken out. The Headmaster is dead, and many of the staff and children are dying. Write a story about how you feel, and the stories and rumours that you might hear.

THE BLACK DEATH: WHAT WAS IT?

Some countries still have plague. **A** shows the leg of an Asian child who has caught the plague. We are not sure why medieval people called it the Black Death. Perhaps it was because one kind of plague caused black swelling.

Scientists did not discover the germ that caused plague until 1894. The germ bred in rats, which it killed even quicker than it killed people. The rats had fleas. The fleas bit people and so passed on the plague germs. **B** shows the plague flea, 3,000 times larger than life. Before this discovery, people thought they caught plague by breathing something in the air. They carried bunches of flowers and herbs to keep the germs away.

Plague became a killer when infection reached the lungs. This was called *pneumonic plague*, because it destroyed the breathing system. People with pneumonic plague could infect others just by breathing on them. *Bubonic plague* did not spread to the victim's lungs, but caused large swellings as the body fought the germs. A similar thing happens when you have spots, blackheads or boils.

In 1348 an Italian writer called Boccaccio was living in Florence. He saw his father die from the plague. He wrote:

C *It began in young children, male or female, either under the armpits or in the groin by swellings, in some to the bigness of an apple, in others like an egg. It also showed itself by black or blue spots on the arms of many, or on their thighs.*

How did you feel when you were last badly ill? Description **D** of how the

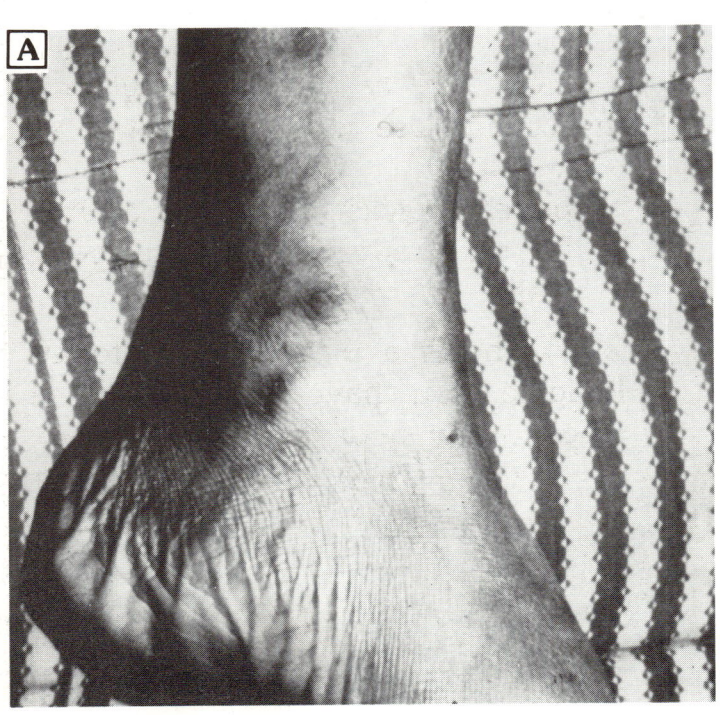

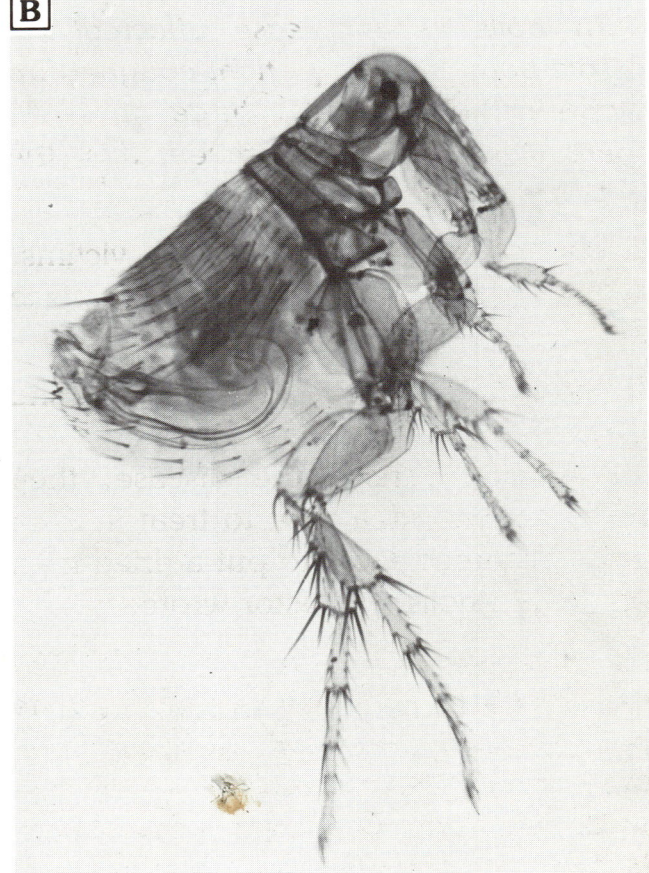

E

plague attacked its victims, was written in 1347 by a priest, Michael of Piazza.

D *Those infected felt pain throughout their bodies. Then boils developed on their thighs or upper arms, about the size of a walnut, which the people called burn boils. The disease affected the whole body and the patient coughed up blood without stop for three days. As there was no way to prevent this, the patient died.*

E shows the burial of plague victims. What suggests that this scene took place in the early stages of the plague?

Doctors tried many ways of curing plague victims. Because doctors did not know what caused the disease, they really had no idea how to treat it. One popular remedy was to put a dried toad on plague boils. A doctor wrote:

F *Toads should be thoroughly dried in the air or sun. They should be laid on the boil. Then the toad will swell and draw the poison of the plague through the skin to its own body. When it is full, it should be thrown away and a new one applied.*

A famous French surgeon, Guy de Chauliac, was the most successful in curing the plague. He realized that there were two forms of plague, and that he could not help victims of pneumonic plague. For victims of bubonic plague, Guy would cut open their boils and burn the wounds with a red-hot iron.

? ? ? ? ? ? ? ? ? ? ? ?

1 Look at E and write a story about the scene. Use these words to help you:

   spades, picks, coffins, monks, shroud, body, mourners, Black Death. ✓

2 ✓ A shows a plague victim today. Imagine you have caught bubonic plague. Say how the disease would affect you. Use these ideas to help you:

   the disease spreads: boils: coughing: temperature: possible cures.

THE BLACK DEATH: LONDON

How did the Black Death affect London? In 1348-49, London was the most important town in Britain for trade, banking and industry. About 60 000 people lived there. **A** and **B** show London streets. Why would it be much unhealthier to live in **A** than **B**? The way the city was built helped the plague to spread. Everybody, rich and poor was crowded together. Usually a family slept in one room. Sometimes up to a dozen people would be asleep on a straw-covered mud floor. Animals slept with them too.

The black rats which spread the plague loved the filth and warmth of the ramshackle wooden houses crammed together inside the city walls (**C**). The streets of London were:

D *lanes, barely wide enough for two donkeys to pass, deep in the mud and filth.*

Black rats feasted on the city's rubbish. People used to throw their rubbish out of windows, onto passers-by. Dead animals

and vegetables rotted in the streets. Little effort was made to get rid of rubbish and sewage. Down the middle of the streets were channels into which people emptied chamber pots and buckets of night soil.

Some privies (toilets) just hung over rivers or streams. At the back of some houses were a private lavatory and cesspool for sewage. The sewage often seeped into wells and fouled drinking water. The black rat bred and multiplied in this environment.

When the plague reached London in the autumn of 1348, it spread like forest fire. A priest wrote:

E . . . . *it killed off many people every day. It spread so much that from the Feast of the Purification (2nd February) till after Easter more than two hundred bodies were buried daily in the new cemetery near Smithfield — to say nothing of other cemeteries. But by the grace of the Holy Spirit, it departed from London at Whitsuntide.*

The priest tells us that about 17 000 to 18 000 Londoners died. We know from church records that three out of seven clergymen in the bishopric of Westminster died in the first half of 1349. Both rich and poor perished. Among the well-off was John Stratford, Archbishop of Canterbury.

The Black Death killed many leading businessmen. The Goldsmiths' Company lost three masters in 1349. The Company of Cutters lost eight masters in one year.

London's population recovered quickly. Peasants who had fled from their villages came there. The new Londoners:

F . . . . *were of all people the most proud and greedy. They disbelieved in God and the old ways of doing things.*

??????????????

1 **C** shows London in 1510 — the first known view. What are **a**, **b**, **c**, **d** and **e**?

2 Look at **A**. Give as many reasons as you can why black rats multiplied in a street like this. Why are there no rats in street **B**? How has it changed since medieval times?

3 Make out a diary as if you were living with a goldsmith's family during the plague in London. Make entries for these dates and events:

1st October 1348: Plague spreads through the city.
1st December 1348: Rumours about dead and dying. You see an open grave.
1st January 1349: Death of the parish priest.
1st April 1349: Plague attacks your parents. They die.
1st June 1349: Rejoicing at the end of the Plague.

THE BLACK DEATH: ITS IMPACT

A shows pilgrims today. They are going to Lourdes, France, where they hope that God will cure them of their illnesses. Medieval people in many countries went on pilgrimages to drive away or curse the plague. A religious band called *flagellants* might have passed your school in 1348-49. They walked in line, beating the person in front with a barbed whip, and praying for help against the Black Death. **B** is a drawing of flagellants.

A common reaction to the plague was to run away, leaving its victims alone. Even families deserted diseased relatives. Often they had no food or drink. Many priests caught the plague. Soon many refused to go into houses to comfort the dying. The Bishop of Bath and Wells complained that:

C . . . . parishes remained altogether without service, and priests left for fear of death.

Things got so bad that men would not enter houses to bury the dead, no matter how much money they were offered. In some villages everyone died or fled. Their huts, hall and church crumbled into ruins. A writer who lived at the time tells us:

D *The price of everything was lower because of the fear of death . . . Sheep and cattle wandered over fields and through crops, with no one to look after them. Crops rotted in the fields because there were no workers to gather them.*

E is an aerial photograph of the site of a deserted medieval village in Buckinghamshire.

What were the final results of the Black Death? About one in three of the labourers and craftsmen of England died. Their deaths meant that much land was no longer farmed. It became overgrown and went back to its wild state. There were not enough workers to go round. Lords and masters could no longer force peasants to work for them. Before the plague, they had been little better than slaves. Now they wanted

more than food and a roof over their heads for their labour. They wanted good wages, or to be given land.

Landowners competed for the few workers left. Those who paid the highest wages got them. Some offered money to get a labourer to leave his master. John Gower, a merchant from Kent wrote:

F *The world goes from bad to worse when shepherd and cowman demand more for their labour than the overseer. Labour is so high priced that those men who employ workers must pay five or six shillings for what used to cost two. Labourers of old did not eat bread made from wheat, their meals were of beans or coarse corn and their drink was water. In those days they knew their place.*

The Black Death hit the Church badly. Many priests died, and there were not enough left to go round. A churchman wrote:

G *Before the plague, for £3 a year a priest would live in a village and hold all the religious services. Now you have to pay up to £20 a year to get anybody to do the job.*

In many monasteries nearly all the monks died. Can you think why?

? ? ? ? ? ? ? ? ? ? ? ? ?

1 On your own drawing of **B** mark who the different people are and what they are doing.

2 In what ways are the pilgrims in **A** different from those in **B**?

3 Before the plague, the deserted medieval village in **E** would have been like the village described in *The Normans*, pages 32-45. Write a report on how the plague affected the village. Discuss:

a The coming of the plague and its spread among the peasant families.
b The flight of many villagers and the death of the priest.
c The state of the fields and animals, the church and houses.
d The end of the plague. The attitude of surviving peasants towards the landowner.

THE PEASANTS' REVOLT: 1

The people in **A** are marching to protest against Britain having the Atomic Bomb.

a Where are they marching to?

b What will they do when they get there?

c What kind of people might help th them?

In 1381 thousands of people joined a protest march to London. A medieval chronicle gives us a clue why:

B *One day just before Whitsun, a tax collector came to the town of Brentwood in Essex . . . . He ordered all the people from nearby villages to come and pay their taxes. They gathered in a crowd and told him that they would not pay. Then the official ordered the sergeant at arms to arrest and imprison these people. But the common folk rose against the royal officials . . . Indeed, they threatened to kill the tax collector.*

The revolt started in Brentwood (see page 20, map **A**) and soon spread across the countryside. Rebels destroyed property, including the home of the King's Treasurer, one of his chief men. In Kent the peasants rose against another royal tax collector. Early in June they captured Rochester Castle. They went on to Maidstone, and chose a local man, Wat Tyler, as their leader. We know little about him. He led the rebels to Canterbury. There they freed a priest called John Ball from the Archbishop's prison.

On 11th June the rebels began their march to London under Wat Tyler and John Ball. As they approached, the king and his courtiers retreated to the tower. Rebels from the surrounding countryside, particularly Essex, were also at the gates of London. At Blackheath, John Ball preached to the peasants. Froissart, a French chronicler who lived at the time, quotes a typical John Ball sermon:

C *My good friends, things cannot go well in England until everyone is equal. Then there shall be neither slaves nor lords, and lords be no more masters than we are. How ill they treat us! For what reason do they keep us in slavery? Are we not all descended from the same ancestors, Adam and Eve? And how can they show why they should be greater masters than ourselves? They are dressed in velvet and other rich cloths, decorated with ermine and other furs, while we are forced to wear rags. They have wines, spices and fine bread, while* we have only black bread and the scraps from the straw. When we drink, it must be water. They have handsome houses and estates, while we must brave the wind and rain to labour in the field. It is by our labour that they have the goods to keep up their pomp. We are called slaves, and if we do not perform our service, we are beaten.

We have no one in authority to whom we can complain or who is willing to hear us. Let us go to the King and argue with him. He is young, and from him we may get a good answer. If not, we ourselves must try to put things right.

The Kent rebels forced their way across London Bridge into London. King Richard II (1377-99) was only fourteen. What was he to do? A writer tells us:

D *He called those lords around him . . . and asked their advice on what should be done in such a crisis. None of them knew, or was willing to advise him.*

A Londoner wrote an account of what happened when a London mob joined the rebels from Essex and Kent:

E *Together they . . . passed straight through the city to the house of Sir John (of Gaunt), Duke of Lancaster, called Le Savoy, and there they turned towards the church of the hospital of St. John of Jerusalem, outside Smithfield, and burnt and levelled nearly all the houses there, except for the church.*

. . . The next morning, all the men from Kent and Essex met at the said place called Mile End, together with some of the faithless persons of the city . . . whose numbers could not be counted. And there the King came to them from the Tower, accompanied by many knights and esquires, and citizens on horseback, the lady his mother also following him in a carriage. There, on the demand of the crazed mob, our Lord the King granted that they might capture those who were traitors against him, and slay them, wherever they might be found.

---

1 Draw a map, and show the possible routes of the Kent and Essex rebels as they marched on London.

2 If you had been with the rebels, what might you have taken on your journey, and what problems and dangers might you have faced?

3 Why did the peasants revolt, and why did they march on London?

4 Read John Ball's sermon carefully. Give a similar account of complaints against your school. How would you go about settling them? Why might you not join the rebels in 1381, or the Ban-the-Bomb marchers in **A**?

5 If you were one of Richard II's advisers at the Council meeting described in **D**, what would you suggest he did? Put plans **a-d** into your order of choice, with reasons.

   a Retreat into the inner tower, with his soldiers.

   b Gather his soldiers, and try to escape into the countryside.

   c Send for help to nobles outside London.

   d Meet Wat Tyler and John Ball, and give in to their demands.

THE PEASANTS' REVOLT: 2

The Londoner explained what happened after the meeting at Mile End:

A *The crazed mob made its way towards the Tower of London, entering which by force, they dragged out Sir Simon (of Sudbury), Archbishop of Canterbury and Chancellor of our Lord the King, and brother Robert Hales . . . the King's Treasurer . . . whom they beheaded at the place called Tower Hill, outside the Tower, and then carried their heads through the city upon lances. They set them up on London Bridge, fixing them on stakes.*

. . . The same day there was no little slaughter in the city, of natives as well as foreigners. Richard Lions, citizen and wine-merchant, and many others, were beheaded in Cheapside. In the Vintry there was a great massacre of Flemings, and in one heap were about forty headless bodies of people who had been dragged from churches and houses. Hardly was there a street in the city in which bodies were not lying. Some of the houses in the said city were pulled down, others in the suburbs destroyed, and some, too, burned.

Look at **B**. What is happening? It shows the end of the Peasants' Revolt described in **C**. On June 15th, King Richard II rode to Smithfield, London, to hear the peasants' complaints. With him were his courtiers and William Walworth, Lord Mayor of London. Henry Knighton, a monk, wrote in his chronicle:

C *The rebel leader, Wat Tyler, approached close to the King, and set out the rebels' demands. He got out his dagger, and tossed it from hand to hand, like a schoolboy playing a game. If the*
rebels' demands were not allowed, it was thought he would stab the King.

The rebels demanded the right to fish where they liked, to catch hares in the fields, and hunt in woods and forests. Only the wealthy could do so at this time.

While the King was thinking about these demands, Tyler went up and threatened him. Wickedly he dared seize the bridle of the King's horse.

A London writer takes up the story:

D *William Walworth, Mayor of London, shouted at Wat (Tyler) on account of his violence and rudeness to the King, and arrested him.*

Wat grew very angry on his arrest, and

stabbed the Mayor in the body with his dagger. But the mayor wore armour, and was not harmed. He drew his own dagger and struck back at Wat. He gave him a deep cut in the neck and a great blow on the head. During the fight, a man of the King's household drew his sword and ran Wat two or three times through the body thus giving him his death wound.

Froissart, the French chronicler, tells us:

E *The uncontrolled mob saw that their leader was dead, and so began to argue: "Our leader is dead. Let's go and kill them all." And they got ready for battle, with their bowmen in front.*

*Alone the King rode up to this mob, who were determined on revenge for their leader's death. The King said, "What is wrong? You will have no leader but me. I am your King. Be calm." (Picture **F**)*

The revolt was now over, and the rebels went home. The King's men acted quickly against the remaining leaders. They caught and hanged many of them. Their bodies were strung up for all to see in towns and villages. John Ball was hanged, drawn and quartered on 15th July 1381.

???????????

1 Draw a cartoon to show what the peasants did in London, *or* tell the story in the form of a newspaper article.

2 Look at **B**.
Who is the man in the long robe on the horse?
Who is the horseman drawing his sword?
Who is the man with the drawn sword in one hand and his other hand on the shoulder of the horseman drawing his sword?

3 Look at **B** and **F**, and say how closely they match accounts **C**, **D** and **E**. Note:
 a The peasants' dress;
 b The killing of Wat Tyler;
 c The position of the mob during the meeting with the King;
 d The background scenery.

4 How trustworthy are **B** and **F**, and **C**, **D** and **E**, as evidence about the end of the Peasants' Revolt?

5 What was it like to be caught up in the Peasants' Revolt? Write a diary as if you were a young person in the mob during the days of revolt. Talk about what you heard, saw, smelt and did, and what feelings you had. Say what you thought about how the revolt ended.

THE HUNDRED YEARS' WAR

Have you seen a football or rugby match between England and France on television? The two countries have played such matches for over a hundred years. Between 1337-1453, the British and French Kings took part in a different kind of contest—war.

They did not fight all the time. Like a football match, the war would suddenly burst into life, in a campaign, battle or treaty. Fortunes swayed from side to side. First one side would be winning, and then the other. Finally, in 1453, the French King managed to drive the English from nearly all the French lands. Only Calais was left in English control—to be lost years later.

What was the war about? Map **A** shows English lands in France in 1337. **B** is a list of reasons why Edward III, King of England (1327-77), decided to fight the French. Edward was a keen soldier and a strong ruler of England.

War began in 1337. In 1340 a sea battle was fought off Sluys, Flanders. About

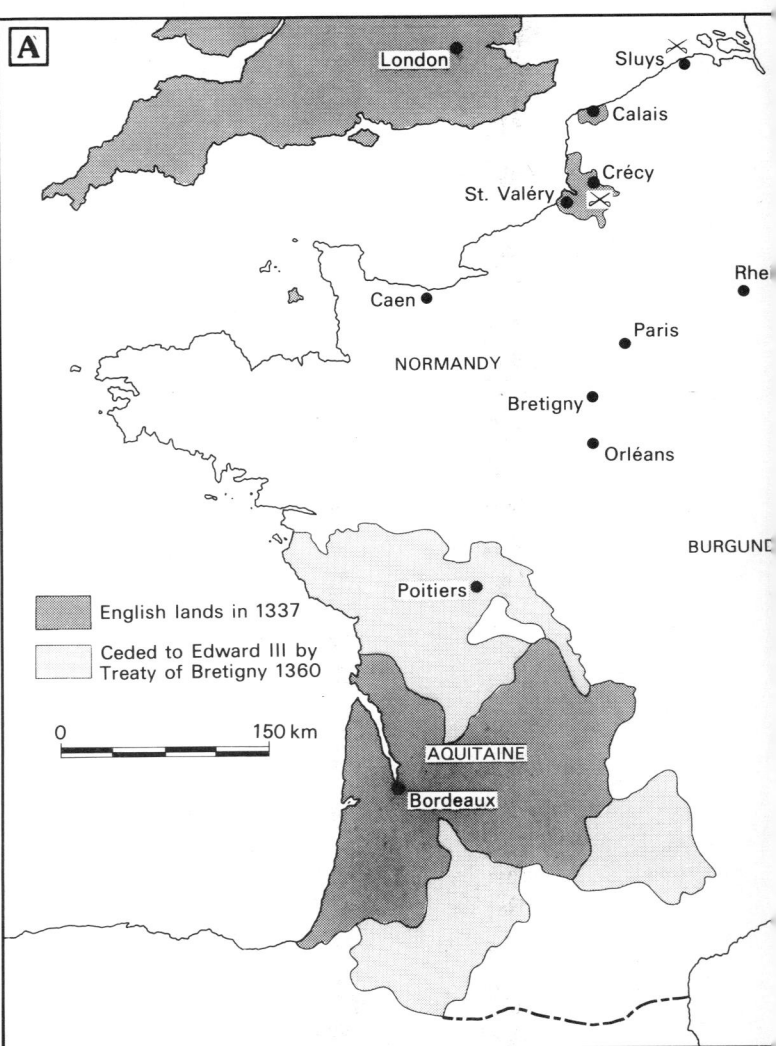

A

English lands in 1337

Ceded to Edward III by Treaty of Bretigny 1360

0   150 km

London · Sluys · Calais · Crécy · St. Valéry · Caen · Rhe · Paris · NORMANDY · Bretigny · Orléans · BURGUND · Poitiers · AQUITAINE · Bordeaux

B

a Edward III claimed that he should also be King of France. The family tree shows why (**C**).

b England's main trade was in wool to Flanders. France was trying to stop this trade. She was also stopping the wine trade between England and Gascony.

c The French had helped Edward III's main enemies at home — the Scots.

d A foreign war would keep Edward III's barons busy. Otherwise they might rebel—as they had against Edward's father, Edward II, whom they murdered in 1327.

200 English ships attacked a larger French fleet at anchor. An English writer, who perhaps talked to men at the battle, tells us:

D *A shower of arrows from long wooden bows so poured on the Frenchmen that thousands died. Finally both sides closed in and came to hand-to-hand blows with pikes, poleaxes and swords. From the top of ships some threw stones that brained their enemies.*

From 1341-46 no major campaigns took place. Both sides mounted raids. In August 1346, Edward III raised a large army of about 12 000 men. He landed in Normandy, captured Caen and marched as far inland as Paris. The French King threatened to surround Edward III. At Crécy, Edward came face to face with

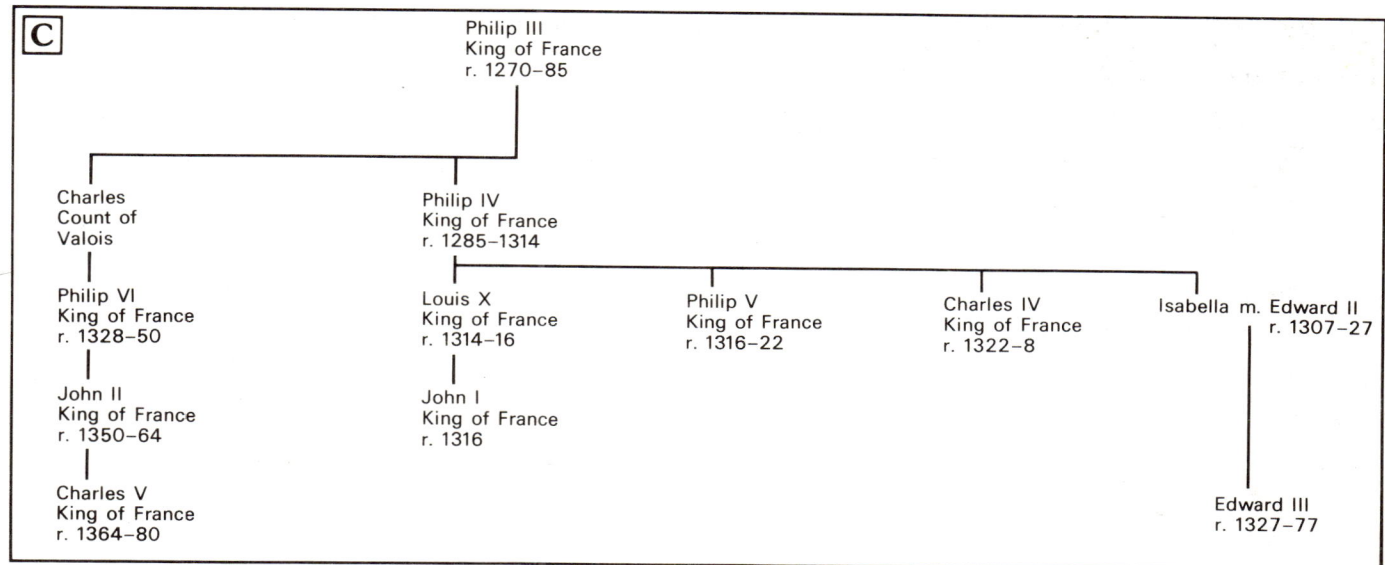

C

Philip III
King of France
r. 1270–85

Charles
Count of
Valois

Philip VI
King of France
r. 1328–50

John II
King of France
r. 1350–64

Charles V
King of France
r. 1364–80

Philip IV
King of France
r. 1285–1314

Louis X
King of France
r. 1314–16

John I
King of France
r. 1316

Philip V
King of France
r. 1316–22

Charles IV
King of France
r. 1322–8

Isabella m. Edward II
r. 1307–27

Edward III
r. 1327–77

the much larger French army. French pikemen and Genoese crossbowmen led an attack on the English lines. A Frenchman wrote:

E *The English archers routed them. They would have fled, but the chief (French) lords did not wait to attack together, but rushed forward in such disorder that the pikemen and Genoese were trapped between them and the English. The weaker soldiers fell on top of those who were trapped, and the others trampled and fell on top of each other in turn, like a litter of piglets.*

The English archers easily managed to shoot the French knights. Crécy was a major French defeat.

In 1347 the English took Calais. In the next few years they raided deep into the French king's lands. In 1356 Edward III's son, the Black Prince, took charge of a raid. The French cut off his army of 6000. At Poitiers, the French king moved in for the kill. French knights on horseback and foot advanced towards the English lines. But then the Crécy fiasco was repeated and the French were utterly defeated. Among the captured French was their King. In 1360, by the Treaty of Brétigny, he surrendered to the English one-third of his French lands.

Small-scale fighting continued for the next sixty years. Slowly the French won back most of the lands lost by the Treaty of Brétigny. By 1370 the Black Prince was too ill to fight, and without a skilled general the English were driven from most of their French lands. Only a few coastal ports like Calais and Bordeaux were left when Edward III died in 1377. It was nearly fifty years before an English king was again willing to fight a major campaign in France.

?????????????

1 Use the evidence on these pages to write your own chronicle about the first half of the Hundred Years' War from the French viewpoint. Make entries for: the causes of the war; the Battle of Sluys; Crécy; the Black Prince and Poitiers; the Treaty of Brétigny; France's fight back.
Or draw a strip cartoon to show how the struggle went between the English and French kings from 1337 to 1377.

2 Put reasons **a**-**d** in table **B** into what Edward III would have thought their order of importance was. Give your reasons.

THE HUNDRED YEARS' WAR: AGINCOURT, 1415

In 1415, King Henry V of England (1413-22) sailed with an army to France. He aimed to win back the English lands in France lost in the previous forty years. In August he landed at Harfleur, which he captured in September. Sickness cut his army in half, and in October he marched inland with only 5000 archers and 900 knights. At Agincourt he came face to face with a much larger French army.

Henry V had with him his private priest, Thomas Elmham, who wrote an account of the battle. It was fought between two woods. The English knights were in the centre of their line, with the archers on each side. The French knights on foot pushed forward towards the English line, and knights on horseback on each flank attacked the archers. Thomas Elmham tells us that the English archers carried:

A . . . *a round or square pole or staff, two metres long, sharp at each end and sufficiently thick (to stop a horse). When the French army came near enough to fight, each archer was ordered to fix his pole in front of him. Their knights attacked our archers on both sides of the army. By God's will they had to retreat quickly because of the shower of arrows . . . . When the opposing knights had nearly reached each other, the French split into three groups. In three places they charged our lines where our flags were, and got their spears tangled up with* ours. *So fierce was their attack that we had to pull back a spear's length. Our men quickly won back the lost ground.*

Both lines of knights were locked together, with more French closing in from the rear. Thomas notes:

B *Our archers cut down the French flanks with their arrows. After they had used up their arrows, they picked up axes, poles, sharp spears and swords. . . They broke up the enemy, felled and stabbed them. Fear and panic seized the French. . . . As men died, those behind pushed forward. The living fell over the dead. At three spots among our main forces, so great grew the mounds of dead and those among them, that our men climbed up the mounds. They were higher than a man.*

News reached Henry V that the French were attacking the rear of his army. He ordered all prisoners to be killed. The news proved false, for the French were beaten.

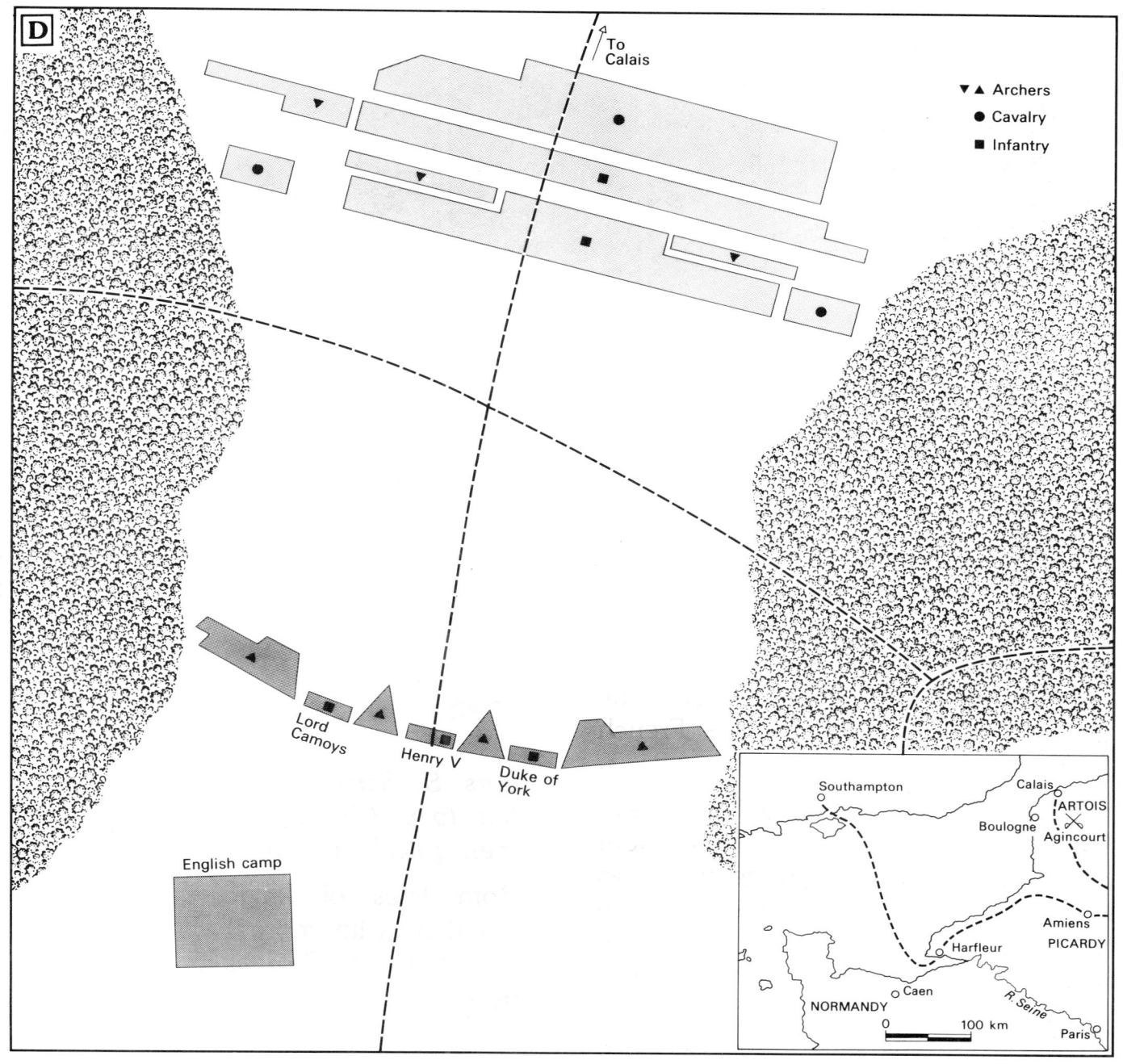

D

To Calais

Archers ▼ ▲
Cavalry ●
Infantry ■

Lord Camoys

Henry V

Duke of York

English camp

Southampton — Calais — ARTOIS — Boulogne — Agincourt — Amiens — PICARDY — Harfleur — Caen — NORMANDY — R. Seine — Paris

0   100 km

---

1 Look at Thomas Elmham's account, **A** and **B**. Then write a story about the Battle of Agincourt. Use these ideas to help you: swords, battle-axes, spears, body armour, helmets, knights on horseback, archers, bows. *Or* mark on a plan of the battle how it went.

2 Look at map **D**, which shows how the English and French armies were drawn up at the start of the battle. How would you advise the French King to draw up his forces? Take into account that:

a knights on foot can only walk very slowly in their heavy armour;

b French archers use cross-bows, which are slow to load and fire;

c knights on horseback are in danger of being mown down by the English archers, with the rapid fire from their bows;

d there are about 6000 English soldiers, and 20000 French.

JOAN OF ARC

Have you heard of Joan of Arc? If so, make a note of what you remember. These pages give some evidence about her. Read them, and see if they add to your idea of her.

Early Life

Joan was born a French peasant's daughter in about 1412 at Domrémy. By 1422, the Hundred Years' War had broken out again, and Charles VII was doing badly. Joan now began to hear the voice of an angel, saying that:

B *I should be at the King's side . . . there was no one else in the whole world, no king, no duke . . . except me who can win back the kingdom of France.*

C

In 1428 Joan went to see the French King (**C**). Charles agreed to see her because he had heard about her. She told him that she would drive the English away from the city of Orléans which they were besieging; and that she would have him crowned as king in Rheims cathedral. This was in English hands. Charles VII had Joan trained as a knight, and put her in charge of a band of soldiers.

Siege of Orléans

Joan arrived at Orléans in March 1429. She helped the defenders capture some English fortifications outside the city. On 7th May she took over the final French attack on the main English fort. If it fell, the English would have to end the siege. The French commander wanted to give up the struggle. Joan's servant later wrote:

D *All those in the maid's force came together, and attacked the fort with such fury that they soon took it, and the enemy fled.*

Joan saved Orléans.

Coronation at Rheims

Joan now persuaded Charles VII to march on Rheims, although his courtiers were against this move. The march to Rheims was a triumph, and The English were expelled. Charles was crowned in the Cathedral. Joan's banner was carried at the head of the coronation procession.

Joan's Death

Joan went on fighting the English. In May 1430 their allies captured her, and handed her over in 1431. The English tried Joan as a witch, and sentenced her to death. On 30th May 1431 she was burned to death at the stake in Rouen market square.

Joan's fight was not in vain, for soon the English had lost all their lands in France except Calais. The English were now kept busy with wars at home over who should be king—the Wars of the Roses.

E

???????????????

1 Look at **A** and **E**. What ideas do they give you about Joan of Arc?

2 Joan of Arc is one of the patron saints of France, as Saint George is a patron saint of England. Make out a table like **F** to say why the French think so highly of Joan of Arc.

F

Evidence	French reasons for thinking her their patron saint
Early life Visit to the King of France Siege of Orléans Coronation at Rheims Joan's death	

3 What modern women have had as much impact on their country's history as Joan of Arc?

THE WARS OF THE ROSES

The cricket match between Yorkshire and Lancashire in the county championship is known as the Roses match. Do you know why? From 1449-85 two noble families quarrelled over which should rule England. The families were those of Lancaster and York (see page 20, map **A**). Their followers wore badges, particularly the red rose of Lancaster and the white rose of York.

The fight for power was long and fierce. First one side and then the other seemed to be winning. But the actual period that the armies spent fighting was short—about sixteen weeks altogether. Table **A** gives the major events and map **A** on page 20 shows the sites of the main battles.

Most of the great landowners of England joined in. Affairs were very confused, for when one side was on top the nobles would change sides, and try and seize the lands and property of other landowners. The problem largely arose because Henry VI (1422-61, 1470-71) was a weak King. Henry was very

A	Date	Main events	Lancaster or York winning	What the Pastons were doing
	1453	Henry VI, Lancastrian King, goes mad. Nobles rule.	L	
	1455	Richard, Duke of York, becomes Protector—rules for Henry VI. Battle of St Albans. Yorkist victory over Henry VI.	Y	
	1459	Battle of Ludford. Yorkists lose.	L	Pastons fail to fight for Henry VI.
	1460	Battle of Northampton. Yorkists win. Duke of York claims throne, but dies in December.	Y	
	1461	Second Battle of St Albans. Yorkists win. Edward, new Duke of York, crowned King Edward IV.	Y	Pastons fight for Edward IV against Lancastrians, and serve him at court.
	1469	Earl of Warwick rebels against Edward IV. Edward captured.	L	Pastons lose Caister Castle to Duke of Norfolk. Growing contempt for Edward IV.
	1470	Edward IV escapes abroad. Henry VI restored to throne.	L	
	1471	Edward IV returns. Battles of Barnet and Tewkesbury. Earl of Warwick and the Lancastrian heir killed. Henry VI dies.	Y	Pastons fight against Edward IV at Barnet.
	1477			Pastons regain Caister Castle.
	1483	Edward IV dies. His brother crowned King Richard III.	Y	
	1485	Battle of Bosworth. Richard III killed. Henry Tudor crowned King Henry VII.	Tudor family takes throne	
	1487	Battle of Stoke. Henry VII wins.		Pastons fight for Henry VII against Yorkists.

religious, and would have preferred to be a monk instead of a king. Because he failed to control his barons, they fought. One of these, the Earl of Warwick, in 1469 was strong enough to remove the Yorkist King, Edward IV, from the throne. Table **A** gives an idea of how a landowning family, the Pastons, was sucked into the contest.

What was life like during the Wars of the Roses? We have clues to what happened in the *Paston Letters*. The Paston family owned land in Norfolk. Margaret Paston ran the family affairs. In the first period of fighting, a powerful neighbour tried to seize the Paston lands at Gresham.

Margaret wrote to her husband, John:

B *. . . . get some crossbows, windacs (grappling irons) to bind them with, and quarrels (arrows for crossbows); for your houses here be so low that no man may shoot with a longbow, though we have ever so great a need.*

. . . I suppose you should get such things from Sir John Fastolf if you would send to him. Also I would like you to get two or three short poleaxes (weapons like hatchets) to keep by the door. . . . Patrick and his men are sore afraid that you will attack them again. They have stored many supplies within the house, and it is said that they have put bars across the doors, and they have made wickets (small windows) on every side of the house to shoot out of, with both bows and hand guns. . . .

When King Edward IV was captured in 1469 (see table **A**), the Duke of Norfolk felt free to use his own troops against the Pastons. Margaret Paston wrote to her son, now head of the family:

C *. . . . your brother and his men stand in great jeopardy at Caister, and lack food, and Daubeney and Berney (knights that the Pastons had hired to*

fight for them) be dead, and many others greatly hurt. They are out of gunpowder and arrows, and the castle is badly broken down by enemy guns. So, they must have speedy help, otherwise they will likely lose their lives and the castle, to the greatest shame to you that ever happened to any gentleman. For, every man in the country is amazed greatly that you suffer them to be so long in jeopardy without help or other remedy.

The Duke has sent for all his tenants from every place, and others, to be at Caister on Thursday next, that there is likely to be the greatest multitude that came there yet. They intend to make a great assault. For they have sent to Lynn for guns, and other places by the seaside. With their great number of guns, shot and other weapons, no man dare appear in the place. . . . It shall not lie in the power of those within (Caister Castle) to hold it.

Margaret suggested that her son should appeal to all the leading noble families for help. He refused, and ordered the men in Caister Castle to surrender.

?????????????

1 Draw on a plan of a castle like Stokesay (see pages 46-47) how you would have made its defences stronger if a noble was about to attack it in the Wars of the Roses, and what you think might happen to it when attacked.

2 Draw up a table showing what steps you would like take to defend your house if the neighbours attacked it. Compare this with a similar table for the defence of Gresham and Caister.

3 Why was the Duke of Norfolk able to capture Caister? How might the Pastons try to get it back?

THE BATTLE OF BARNET, 1471

The battle was over. Jack Paston wrote home:

A . . . blessed be God, my brother John is alive and fares well, and in no peril of death. Nevertheless he is hurt, with an arrow in his right arm, beneath the elbow.

John and Jack Paston had been fighting for the Earl of Warwick and the Lancastrians. They were against King Edward IV and the Yorkists. The Pastons were angry because in 1469 the King had failed to stop the Duke of Norfolk from seizing the Pastons' castle at Caister. In 1470 King Edward lost his throne and fled abroad, when some of his powerful noble supporters deserted to his Lancastrian enemies.

In 1471 Edward returned to England to win back the throne. He captured London, where he learned that Warwick's army was marching towards him. So King Edward moved his army to Barnet to meet them. Map **B** shows where the armies stood at the start of the Battle. At the end of the Battle, one of King Edward'sservants wrote how the King had drawn up his men during the night.

C And, because it was very dark, and he could not see well where his enemies were drawn up, he placed himself and all his men in front of them, much nearer than he supposed. Also, he did not make these arrangements as he would have liked, if he could have seen (the enemy) better, but somewhat askew. He kept his men in good order, all that night, so that they kept still, without any talking or noise.

Warwick's guns opened fire, but their shot passed over the heads of Edward's men. John and Jack Paston were on the right of Warwick's army, with the Earl of Oxford's force—map **B**. As dawn broke, Edward's servant tells us:

D . . . between four and five of the clock, notwithstanding a great mist that stopped them seeing one another, he (King Edward) committed his cause and quarrel to almighty God, advanced his banner and blew on his trumpets. They set upon them (the enemy), first with shot, and then, soon, they joined in hand-to-hand fighting.

John and Jack Paston's force overran Hastings' small force, that faced it on the left of Edward's army. Edward's servant tells us:

E . . . many fled towards Barnet, and so forth to London. But . . . the rest of the armies . . . could not see that distress, nor the fleeing, nor the chase, because

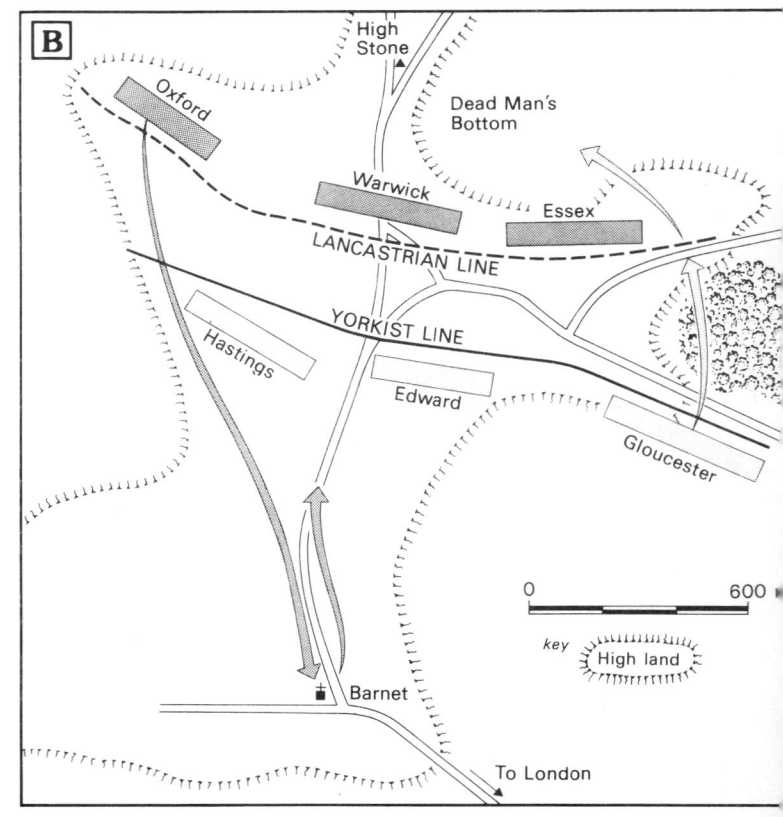

F

of the great mist . . . and so the King's army was thereby in nothing discouraged.

King Edward was in a desperate mess. He faced the main part of Warwick's army. The Earl of Gloucester's force—see map **B**—could only fight a few of the enemy. Luck now played a big part. As mist cleared, Oxford's force, with John and Jack Paston, rode back from the chase to the battlefield. Edward's and Warwick's men were locked in hand-to-hand fighting, as in **F**, drawn about ten years later. Both King Edward and the Earl of Warwick mistook Oxford's banners for those of troops coming to help Edward. Warwick's men turned and fled. Jack Paston's letter tells us:

G *There was killed upon the field, half a mile from Barnet, on Easter Day, the Earl of Warwick.*

The main threat to Edward IV was over. But he had still to defeat another enemy. Edward did this at Tewkesbury, where he killed the son of the previous king,

Henry VI. Edward's enemies now had no one whom they could back against him.

The Pastons were lucky. King Edward pardoned them for fighting against him. They could return to Norfolk in peace, and keep their houses, castles and estates.

The Wars of the Roses came to an end in 1485, when Henry Tudor killed Richard III (1483-85) at the Battle of Bosworth. Henry established a new ruling family, the Tudors, whose members were to be kings and queens of England for the next hundred years.

? ? ? ? ? ? ? ? ? ? ? ? ? ?

1 Look at **F**. List the different weapons and armour, and say how they were used.

2 If you had been with Jack and John Paston when they returned to the battlefield after routing Hastings' force—see map **B**—what thoughts might have gone through your mind? Use these points to help you:

The start of the battle; your charge; hand-to-hand fighting; screams; wounds; John Paston's wound; neighing horses; blood; the enemy's flight; the chase; killings; getting back together; return to the battlefield; seeing Edward's and Earl of Warwick's armies; your hopes.

3 Use map **B**, picture **F** and the written evidence to write your own story of the battle as if you had been with Jack Paston.

4 Why did Edward IV pardon the Pastons?

5 How much trust can an historian put in the evidence on these pages?

THE KNIGHT

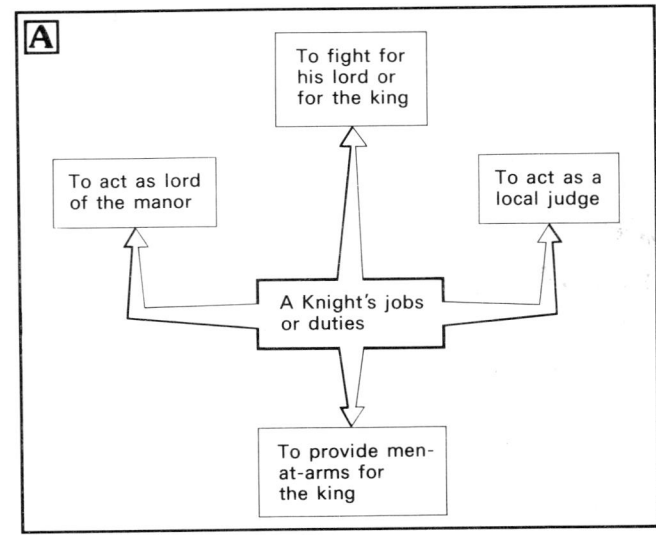

If, in the Middle Ages, your father had been a knight, what jobs would he have had? Diagram **A** gives some ideas. Most of the time he lived on the lands that his lord let to him. Your father *held* these from his lord—one of the king's nobles. In return for these lands, or his *manor* or *fee*, your father promised to fight for his lord when asked. If he could not do so, he had to pay money, *scutage*, instead. Your father and his lord often had to campaign for the king, from whom the lord in turn *held* his lands.

A knight always had to be ready to go and fight. For an idea of knights in battle, see pages 34-35. How did they keep fighting fit? Practice at home was not enough. *Tournaments* were a great help: see **B** and **C**. Here knights fought mock battles in the lists, for prizes. They also charged one another on horseback, which they called a *course*. *Jousting* was fighting with lances. The knights also fought all together, in a huge *melée*. At the end of the contest, those still on their horses were the winners. **D**, written in the Middle Ages, tells how a knight, Ipomydon, fought in a tournament.

D *Plenty of great knights came there, dressed for the tournament. A thousand were present, armed with lance and sword. Knights began to fight. On all sides they were unhorsed. That day Ipomydon was victorious. There he ran many a course. With his lance he struck all he met, and flung both horse and rider to the ground. The judges gave him the prize—a thousand pounds.*

How did the judges recognize Ipomydon in the melée? Knights had their own badges on their shields—see **E**—and on

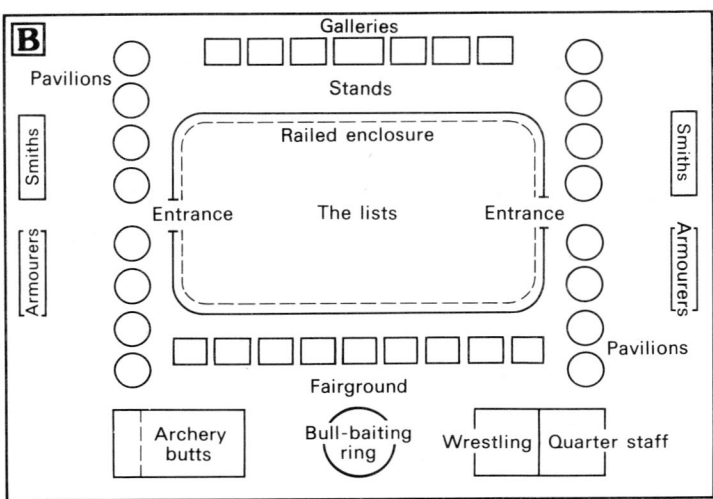

the flags *pennons*, at the end of their lances. *Heralds* designed and coloured these badges, according to clear rules. We call these rules *heraldry*.

By about 1450, your father's armour would have slowly changed from Norman chain-mail to heavy plate. **F** and **G** give you some idea of how it evolved. As a knight, your father treated women with great respect. Sometimes he won the favour of a lady—not always your mother. In tournaments and battles he fought for her honour. Often she gave him a small present, such as a handkerchief, to wear in his helmet. This was a token of his lady's regard.

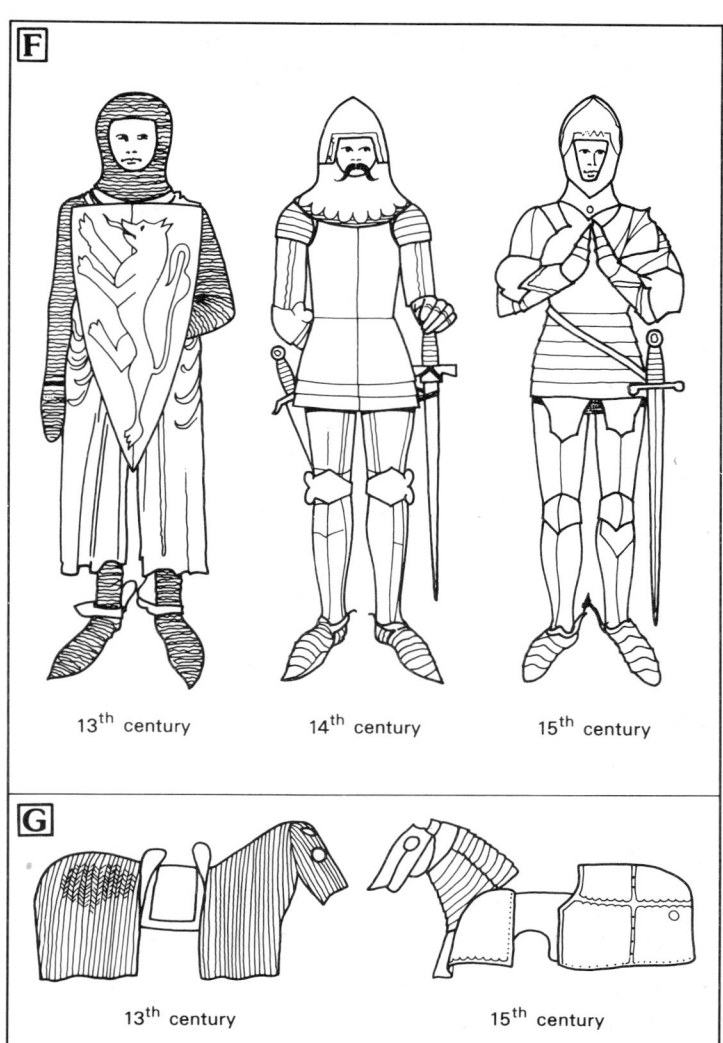

F

13th century   14th century   15th century

G

13th century   15th century

E

?????????????????????????

1 If you attended a tournament, what would you see at these spots:
the lists; archery butts; quarter staff; armourers; farriers; bull-baiting ring?

2 In the evening in the castle hall, knights told stories about their deeds in tournaments, battles and campaigns. Tell a story about Ipomydon, using the evidence on these pages. Use these words to help you:
fee; scutage; jousting; course; melée; pennon; heraldry; honour.

3 If in about 1450 you went to buy armour for a knight, what would you order? Make out a table like this.

Part to be protected	Armour needed	How made
Head and neck		
Arms		
Body		
Legs and feet		
Horse		

4 How did armour change between 1200 and 1400? Why do you think it evolved in this way?

5 Looking at **E**, try to work out how heralds designed shields to make sure that no knight had the same pattern as another.

PAGE AND SQUIRE

If you want to be a soldier when you leave school, how will you go about it? What will the job be like? What weapons will you have? How will you be trained to use them?

If you were a boy and lived in the Middle Ages, and became a soldier who fought in armour on horseback—a knight—how would you have been brought up? You would probably have been the son of a knight. At about the age of eleven or twelve, you might have been sent to be a page—the servant of a lord that your father knew. **A** and **B** are evidence about a page's life. In **A** the writer tells of his own life as a page in about 1306.

A *Often I have made from a stick a horse called Grisel. We used to make helmets of our hats; and often, in front of the girls, we beat one another with our caps. . . . I amused myself night and morning with a spinning top, and I've often made soap bubbles in a little pipe, two or three, or four or five. I loved to watch them. When I was a little older, I had to behave myself, for they made me learn Latin. If I made mistakes in saying my lessons, I was beaten, or, being afraid of being beaten, I did better. However, once away from my teacher, I could never rest until I fought with the other boys. I was beaten and I beat. I was so knocked about that often my clothes were torn. When I got home, I was told off and hit again.*

C is a picture of Chaucer's squire from a medieval book of his poems.

At about fourteen you became a squire. Already you had learnt much about knighthood. Now you began to live like a knight and practise with real weapons, as in picture **D**. In about 1380, the poet Chaucer (see pages 54-55) wrote about a:

E *. . . fine young squire,*
A lover and a likely lad, a ball of fire,
With snaky locks that seem to have been curled.
Some twenty years of life he'd unfurled,
In height he was not all that very long,
But mighty nimble and amazing strong.
He'd fought abroad with a band of knights
In Flanders, Artois and Picardy's heights.
And yet in time of so very little space
He'd done ever so well—winning a lady's grace.
His clothes embroidered like a meadow bright

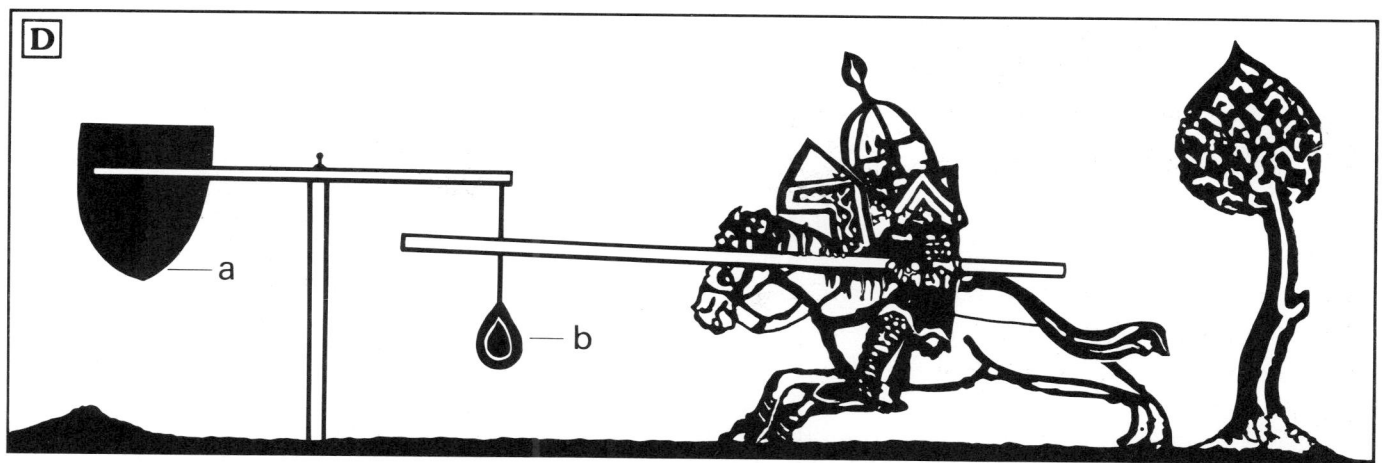

Practice. The aim was to hit shield **A**. What was the point of weight **B**?

Full of fine flowers, so fresh, so red, so white.
He sang, or played the flute throughout the
day —
He was as fresh as is the month of May.
His gown was short with sleeves both long
and wide,
And on a horse knew he always how to ride.
Poems and songs he'd made, and them recite.
He knew to dance, to joust, to draw and write.

If a squire fought bravely in battle, his lord might make him a knight straight away. The squire knelt and his lord dubbed him on the shoulder with the flat of his sword, **F**. Or, if the squire lived with his lord for five years and did well he might take his vows of knighthood. He promised to be a good Christian and behave like a true knight—**G**.

These are three connecting pictures. **a** The squire of a young knight holds his shield and pennon. **b** The squire helps the knight to dress. **c** The king ties on the knight's sword, while his squire puts on his spurs.

??????????????

1 Draw a table comparing a day in your life with the day of a page or young squire in the Middle Ages. Put activities that are alike side by side.

Page's life	Your life
. . . .	. . . .
. . . .	. . . .

2 Write a poem like **E** about the squire shown in **C**.

3 Use the evidence on these pages to say what kind of things a young man had to do to become a knight.

THE KNIGHT'S DAUGHTER

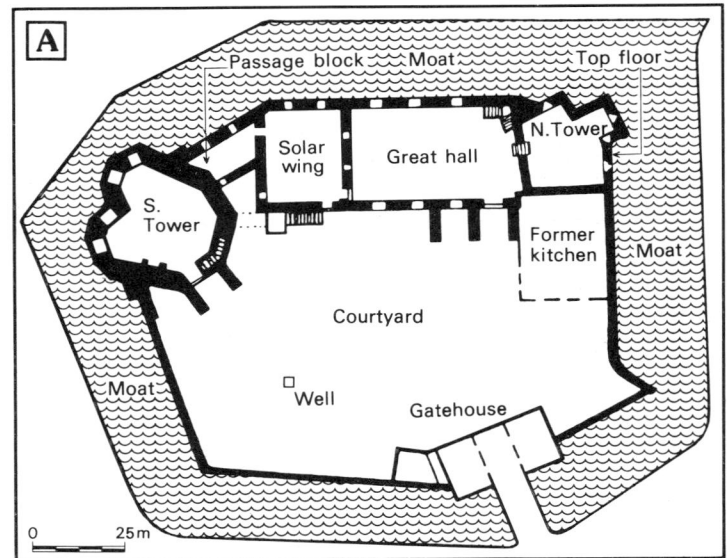

Do you help your mother do the housework and cooking? What would home life have been like if you were a knight's daughter in 1380? By then, many a knight had turned his manor house into a fort. It served as both castle and a home. One of these, **A**, survives at Stokesay in Shropshire (see page 20, map **A**). **B** shows the Great Hall from the inside, and **C** the outside of the Great Hall. **D** is a medieval account of a manor.

D . . . *a handsome hall with a good oak ceiling. On its west side a splendid bed. On the ground level a stone chimney, a toilet and another small room. At the east end is a pantry and wine and beer store. . . . There are four trestle tables in the hall. . . . There is a good kitchen, well covered with tiles, with a huge fire and ovens, one large, the other small for cakes. Alongside the kitchen is a small house for baking. A new granary is divided into a dairy, and covered with oak tiles. Also a henhouse. . . . These buildings are enclosed in a moat, a wall and a hedge. Beyond the outer gate is a pigsty.*

In the morning you would get up and dress. You would help your mother give orders to the servants. They would clean, make beds, wash clothes and pots, and cook bread (**E**) and meals (**F**). Then you might go hunting with your father and mother, using hawks and hounds. At night you might have a feast in the Great Hall. About 1380 a writer recorded:

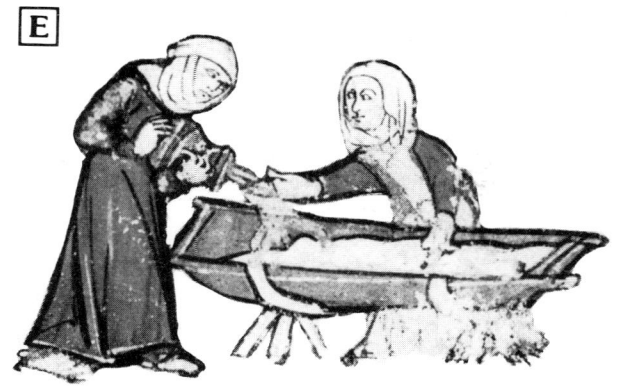

Mixing and making bread

G *Firstly, for a feast, meat is got ready. . . . In the hall, benches, stools and tables are laid out, and towels and cloths put on hand. Then the guests are called together, and seated in order. The lord has chief place at the table. They do not sit down at table before the guests have washed their hands. Children sit in their own place, and servants at a table of their own. First knives, spoons and salt are set on the table, and then bread, drink and many different dishes. Busily household servants help each other to everything, and talk merrily together. The guests are entertained with lutes and harps. Then wine and dishes of meat are brought out and eaten. At the end come fruit and spices. After eating, tablecloths and scraps are taken away, and guests wash and wipe their hands again. Men finally say goodnight. Some stay here to sleep, and some go home to their own beds.*

The food was served on thick slices of bread called trenchers. After the feast the servants and the lord's fighting men would go to sleep on the rush or straw-covered floor. As a knight's daughter you would sleep in a bed—perhaps with a feather, straw or horsehair mattress.

???????????????

1 Make a diary entry for a day in the life of a knight's daughter in June 1380. Use these ideas to help you: getting up and dressing; orders to the servants; a walk around the manor house, visiting all the rooms and other building; what the servants were doing.

2 Have you ever been to a fancy-dress party? Imagine holding a medieval banquet for your friends. Use the evidence on these pages to make it as realistic as possible.

3 How useful is the evidence on these pages for us to reconstruct the life of a knight's daughter? Make a list like this.

Evidence A
Type of evidence (e.g. photograph, medieval drawing)
What does it tell us?
How reliable is it?

F

quel vous a gmande

THE MERCHANTS AND THE STAPLE

If you visited the House of Lords, you would see the bulky object in Picture **A**. When Parliament meets, the Lord Chancellor sits on it. It is called the Woolsack, for it is a square sack stuffed with wool and covered with red cloth. It reminds us that in the Middle Ages most of England's trading wealth came from selling wool and wool cloth. A medieval poet tells us:

B *O wool, noble dame, thou art the goddess of merchants; to serve you all are ready; by your good fortune and your wealth, you make some rise high, and others bring to ruin.*

One merchant put this verse in the window of his house:

C *I thank God, and ever shall,*
it is the sheepe, hath paid for all.

The Black Death caused a big change in farming. Because of the drop in the number of peasants, many landlords used their land for raising sheep or cattle. This needed fewer men than growing crops did.

Before 1350, foreign merchants bought most English wool to sell abroad. They exported six out of every ten bales. As late as 1480, an English wool merchant, Richard Cely, moaned:

D *Nor have I bought this year a lock of wool, for the Italians have bought up the wool of Cotswold.*

King Edward III (1327-77) tried to raise money by controlling the wool trade. He set up what we call the *Staple*. A group of merchants got from the king the right to export all wool through one port. The

A

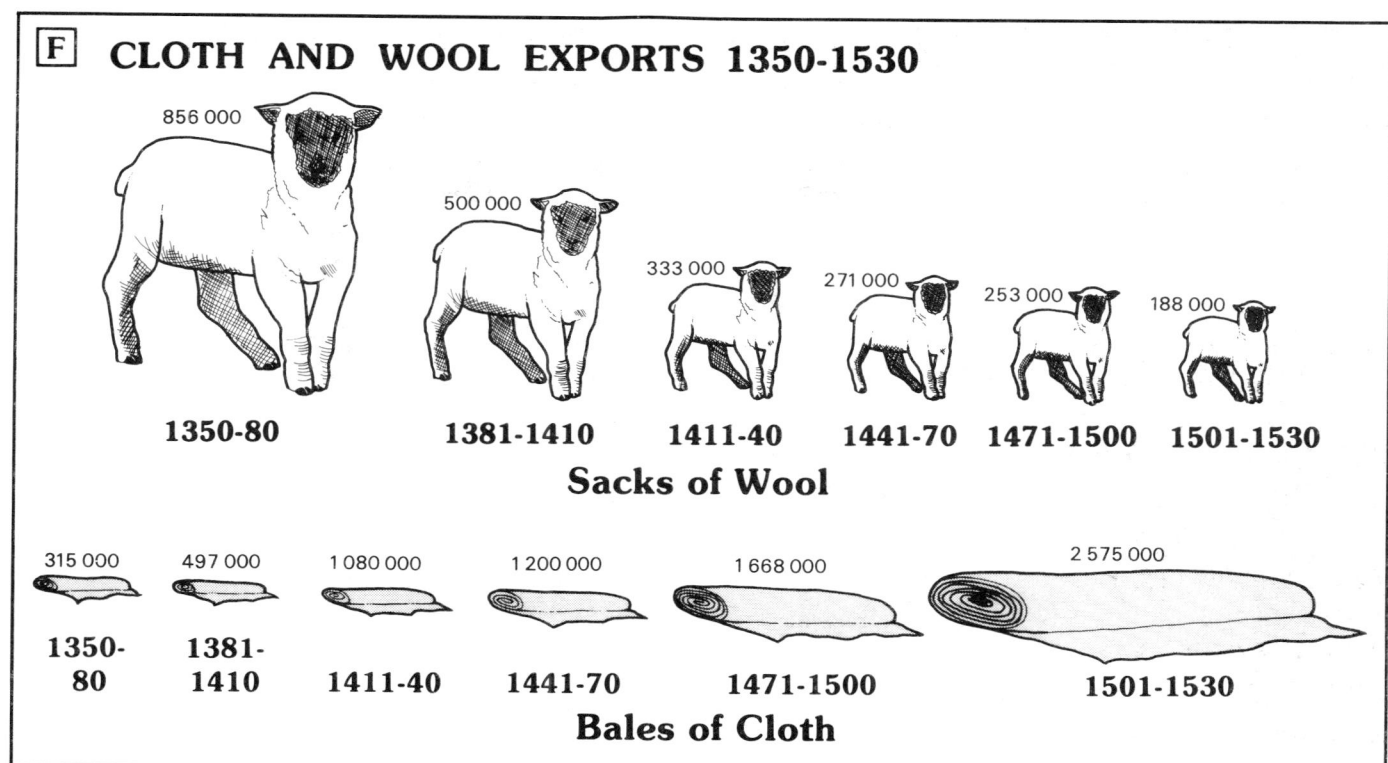

F CLOTH AND WOOL EXPORTS 1350-1530

Sacks of Wool

856 000	500 000	333 000	271 000	253 000	188 000
1350-80	1381-1410	1411-40	1441-70	1471-1500	1501-1530

Bales of Cloth

315 000	497 000	1 080 000	1 200 000	1 668 000	2 575 000
1350-80	1381-1410	1411-40	1441-70	1471-1500	1501-1530

merchants who bought this monopoly were called *Staplers*. There were about 400 of them. In each district, farmers had to sell their wool in the Staple town. The Staplers changed the Staple port at intervals, for example from Calais to Bruges or Antwerp. The Staple was first fixed at Calais in 1363, and ended up there in 1423.

By the mid-15th century, the Staplers ran all trade in wool, woollen goods, sheepskins, hides and leather. They chose a council of merchants to run their affairs. The Staple had many advantages. One was that the Staplers' ships sailed in a convoy. This meant that they could fight off attacks by pirates. A Stapler's servant wrote from France:

E *Sir, the Wool ships be come to Calais all except three, whereof two be in Sandwich haven, and one is at Ostend, and he has thrown all his wool overboard. On the 27th February came a ship from Dover, and on the Thursday before came forth a vessel from Dover to Calais. She was chased by French ships and driven to Dunkirk to shelter.*

By 1500 the wool trade had changed from exporting bales of wool to exporting wool spun and woven into wool cloth.—See **F**.

?????????????

1 Design a sign for an inn that merchants of the Calais Staple used.

2 Imagine going with a merchant in wool to buy wool. Tell of your journey to the Staple Town, buying the wool, sending it to the Staple Port and the trip across the Channel.

3 Write a story telling why the changes shown in **F** happened to the wool trade between 1350-1530.

4 Near where you live, you should find clues about the wool trade—names of inns, public buildings in towns, churches. Find out as much as you can about clues like this, and their links with the wool trade.

THE WOOL MERCHANTS

A staple merchant was an important man. Often he was the most powerful person in a town, and perhaps its mayor. Evidence about the wool merchants survives in old towns. In churches you can find statues, monuments and brasses—**A**—made in their memory. Some of their houses still stand—**B** and **C**. Letters, accounts and wills tell us much about them. Thomas Betson was a famous merchant. In his will we find:

D *I bequeath* (give) *thirty pounds for the garnishing* (decorating) *of the Staple church in Our Lady's Church at Calais—to buy some jewels, and twenty pounds to the stockfish-mongers* (guilds) *to buy plate.*

The main business of the staple merchant was to buy wool from English sheepfarmers to sell abroad. In the spring and autumn, a wool merchant visited all the wool-growing areas. Often local traders bought wool direct from farmers to sell to Staple merchants. One visiting the Cotswolds (see page 20, map **A**) wrote:

E *Your letter advises me to buy wool in Cotswold. I shall have from John Cely his load of thirty sacks, and from William Midwinter of Northleach forty sacks. I am advised to buy no more as the wool in Cotswold is a great price. . . .*

Other merchants bought wool from the Yorkshire monasteries, whose monks owned huge flocks of sheep. **F** is from a letter that a rich wool merchant, Richard Cely, wrote to his son George:

F *By the grace of God, I am busy shipping 29 samples* (an amount of wool) *which I bought from William Midwinter of Northleach, as the wool packer William Breton told me, and also three samplers of the rectors, which is fair wool.*

When a merchant had bought his wool, he sent it to the coast. There it was loaded in ships and exported. Merchants' letters and the list of customs duties that they paid tell us about the trade:

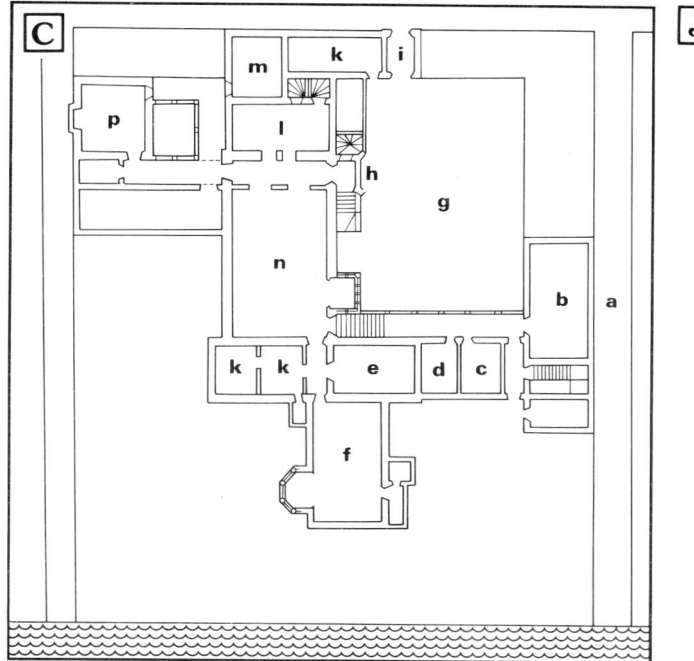

C

a	Water gate
b	cloth house
c	parlour
d	counter
e	chapel
f	great parlour
g	entrance court
h	porch
j	gate
k	chamber
l	buttery
m	butter house
n	hall
p	kitchen

G *Sirs, I am writing to tell you that my master has shipped his wool at the Port of London at this October shipping. In The Mary, William Sordyvale master, is 7 packs, in The Christopher of Rainham, Henry Wylkyns master, 7 packs. Some 3000 pelts lie before the mast, and under them lie 200 sheepskins of Walter Fyldes. . . .*

Officials who collected customs duties made a careful list of all wool exported to the Staple port. When the wool arrived there, the wool merchants paid their duties. They then sold it to European traders—either at the Staple port or another European city, like Bruges or Antwerp. This letter tells us a little about Thomas Betson.

H *Thomas Betson, wool merchant, came into Calais the last day of April and left in good health unto Bruges market the first day of May.*

Northleach Church, Glos., rebuilt by Thomas Fortey, wool merchant, before he died in 1348.

Both during their lives and in their wills, many wool merchants gave money to build, extend and decorate their local churches (**J**). Many of these churches still stand as monuments to the wool merchants.

? ? ? ? ? ? ? ? ? ? ? ?

1 **A**-**J** are evidence about wool merchants. Make out a table showing what each piece of evidence tells you about the wool merchant who had it made.

Evidence A Ideas . . . .
Evidence B Ideas . . . .

2 Imagine you were Thomas Betson writing in a letter to a friend. Use the evidence on these pages, and on pages 48-49, to say what kind of person he was. Use these ideas to help you:

> his job; how he spent the year; how he spent money; his gifts to the church.

3 Use plan **C** of the merchant's house, to work out what each room was for.

THE GUILDS

Medieval guilds were clubs or societies that protected their members. They were rather like trade unions. Members of a particular guild usually worked in their own skilled trade or profession. Members played an important part in town life. **A** and **B** show two sides of guild life that survived.

There were two kinds of guild. One was mainly concerned with the Church and religion. These guilds arranged religious processions and events. Sometimes a guild paid a priest to pray for its members and burn special candles in the guild's own chapel in a church.

C *The tanners' guild decided that they would find a wax candle to burn before Our Lady in All Hallows church near London wall. Also, that each person of the trade shall put into the box such sum as he shall think fit in aid of keeping up the candle.*

These guilds gave money to sick or old members. The rules of the tanners' guild said:

D *Also, if by chance any one of the said trade shall fall into poverty, whether through old age or because he cannot work . . . he shall have every week from the said box 7 pence for his support, if he be a man of good reputation.*

The second kind of guild was mainly concerned with making or selling things. These were the merchant or craft guilds. They too were very religious. Merchant guilds formed soon after the Norman Conquest. These guilds needed a charter from the King. When a town received a royal charter to form a merchant guild, only members of that guild

The procession of the Vinter's Company after the election of a new master

Fishmongers' Comp.y

ALL WORSHIP BE TO GOD ONLY

London.

were allowed to sell guild goods freely in the town. All outsiders had to pay tax on goods that they wanted to sell. In 1347, the rules of the hatmakers' guild of London said:

E *No man shall make or sell any manner of hats within the boundaries of this city if he is not a free man from the said city.*

Guilds had very strict rules about buying and selling their goods. They made sure that quality and price were kept up in the town. Members who broke the rules were punished. Sometimes they even had to leave the guild. In 1429, a shoemakers' guild punished a member:

F *In the city of Chester a shoemaker, William Guidd, was fined the sum of ten pounds by the guild warden for very poor workmanship. Also all his goods were forfeit.*

The merchant guilds included a huge number of different crafts and trades—**G**. Later, each craft set up its own guild. Members chose their officers. The most important was the warden. His job included checking the quality of members' work, and testing apprentices

before they passed out as craftsmen. To become a guild member, you first had to be an apprentice under a master craftsman. He taught you the trade.

H *No one shall be an apprentice in the said trade for a term less than seven years, and that without fraud or trickery. . . . No one who has not been an apprentice or has not finished his term of apprenticeship in the said trade, shall be made free to practise.*

Towards the end of the Middle Ages, the London guilds changed altogether. Only rich merchants were allowed to join. Guilds were then called livery companies. Many livery companies still exist. On special occasions members wear their uniform or livery.

? ? ? ? ? ? ? ? ? ? ? ?

1 In Picture **A**, an apprentice is at work. *Either* draw him, to show what he is doing, *or* in your own words describe the scene. How do you think it might have changed since the Middle Ages?

2 Make a list of the different things that medieval guilds did. Then draw up a list of what modern trade unions do. In what ways are the lists alike, and in what ways are they different?

3 Imagine you were an apprentice in the stonemasons' guild in the Middle Ages. Suppose you are building a church. Make a diary of what happened during a week's work under the master mason.

4 Write as short a story as you can to show what *all* these terms mean:
guild, guild chapel, craft guild, charter, warden, apprentice, master craftsman, livery company.

PILGRIMAGES

Is there anywhere, in England or abroad, that you would really like to visit? Can you say where, and why? In the Middle Ages, people used to go on long journeys to holy places. Of these *pilgrimages*, the two most important were to Rome and Jerusalem. Can you think why? England had many *shrines* for pilgrims, such as the shrine of Thomas Becket at Canterbury—see pages 4-5. A famous poem, *The Canterbury Tales*, tells of a band of pilgrims on a journey from London to Canterbury. The poet was Geoffrey Chaucer, 1340-1400, who worked at court and was a Member of Parliament. He set his tales in April.

A *When people yearn to go on pilgrimages,*
And pilgrims long to see those far-off places
Of distant saints, adored in strangest lands.
And specially, from every county's bounds
In England to Canterbury their ways they bend
To find the holy blessed saint, who'll end
With help their sickness, and soon them mend.
It happened in that season that one day
In Southwark, at the Tabard, as I lay
Ready to go on pilgrimage and start

For Canterbury, most devout at heart,
At night came there into that same pub
Some nine and twenty members of a club
Of different folk, happening then to fall
In friendship, and they were pilgrims all.

Chaucer's pilgrims agreed to tell one another tales on the journey, to pass the time. Each told two on the way there and two on the way back. These make up *The Canterbury Tales*.

B is a medieval picture of Chaucer's pilgrims. **C** shows a similar band. You can read about the knight and squire on pages 42-45, the monk, nun and friar on pages 58-59 and the merchant on pages 48-49. Another of the party was a *yeoman*—a small landowner.

D *This yeoman wore a cloak and hood of green,*
His peacock-feathered arrows were bright and keen,
And neatly sheathed, down from his belt they hung.
For sure his dress the yeoman's praises sung.
His arrows never drooped their feathers low
And in his hands he held a mighty bow.
Brown was his face and head most like a nut
Wherein one found all woodcraft had been shut.
A hardened brace fixed on his arm to ward
Away the bow string, while a shield and sword
Hung at one side, and on the other swayed
A dagger—spear sharp, and most well displayed.

E shows Chaucer's miller.

F *The miller was a man of sixteen stone*
A great stout fellow of muscle and bone.
From then he did mighty well. He'd go
And win the ram at any wrestling show.
Rock hard, and in shoulders broad and square
To break down any door he'd proudly swear,
Or take a run and smash it with his head.
His beard, like that of sow or fox, was red,
And mighty broad as though it was a spade.
On very tip of nose one found displayed

A wart on which a tuft of hair stood out
As red as bristles on an old sow's snout.
His nostrils were as black as they were wide.
He walked with a sword and shield by his side.
His mouth was like a mighty furnace door.
A foul-mouthed scoundrel, in his mind he bore
His dirty tales, that from the gutter leapt.
A master's hand had he that handling corn
                                much kept,
He rolled it with his thumb and so he knew
Its true worth—and then took times three what
                                due.
By God, his thumb of gold judged every sack!
Blue hood, white cloak wore he upon his back.

? ?

1 Write a poem like **F** to describe anyone you have been on holiday with.

2 What was it like to go on a pilgrimage in 1380 from London to Canterbury? It took about ten days. Make out a list like this, with your answers to each point. Use a modern map to help you.

a Why are you going?
b How do you travel? On foot or horseback?
c What clothes are you taking?
d How much food and money do you need?
e Where do you stay?
f How do you pass the time?
g What do you do when you get there?

3 How useful is Chaucer's poem as evidence about medieval pilgrims?

4 Look carefully at **B** and **C**, and make up a story or a scene in a play about them. Say who they were, what they were saying and doing, and where they were going.

THE MONASTERY

Are you fed up? Do you hate school? Do you ever think that you would like a completely different kind of life? How would you like the one in **A**? It lays down rules, like school rules, for boys entering a monastery to become monks in the Middle Ages.

A *Let his parents bring the boy to the altar and wrap his right hand in the altar cloth. Then, having kissed it, let them put it into the hands of the monk who is looking after the boy, and make the sign of the Cross over his head. Then let the Abbot (head of the monastery) pour holy water on the boy's head and cut his hair with the scissors around his neck. Mean-* *while the monk in charge of singing (the precentor) chants the psalm,* Preserve Me, O God. *Now let the boy take off his own clothes and be clothed in the monk's cloak and hood, while the Abbot says, "May the Lord clothe you!"*

D *We are now going to set up a home to serve God. In it will be nothing harsh or a burden . . . We will never leave His home, but stay there until we die.*

When anything that matters has to be decided in the monastery, let the Abbot call all the monks together. After hearing the advice of our brothers (the monks), let him make up his own mind. Let the brothers give their advice humbly . . . Quickly they must obey commands, as they have agreed that the Abbot should rule them.

Eight times a day let us praise our Creator. That is, at Vigils, Lauds, Prime, Tierce, Sext, None, Vespers and Compline.

All the monks shall sleep in separate beds. If possible let them sleep in a bedroom together (a dormitory). Let a candle always burn in the room until morning. Let the monks sleep in their clothes and girdles.

They shall always be ready to rise quickly when the signal is given to hurry to the divine service. . . . And let them rouse the sleepy heads and help them get up.

No one shall keep anything as his own: no *book, writing tablet nor pen. Nothing at all.*

The brothers are to serve each other, so that no one can get out of work in the kitchen. He who ends his weekly work on Saturday must clean everything. He must wash the towels with which the brothers wipe their hands and feet. He who finishes his work, and he who begins, are to wash the feet of all the rest.

Monks shall be silent at all times (except for essential conversation), especially at night. So, on coming from Compline, no one shall speak at all.

Let the brothers be given clothes that suit the weather. . . . In normal places a cloak (habit) and hood (cowl) will be enough for each monk. In winter the habit will be of thicker cloth. He should also have a scapular (apron) to work in, and shoes and stockings. Monks must not grumble about the colour or rough cloth of their dress. When getting new, they must always give back the old to be kept for the poor. Two habits and two cowls are enough for a monk. A mattress, blanket, sheet and pillow are enough for a bed.

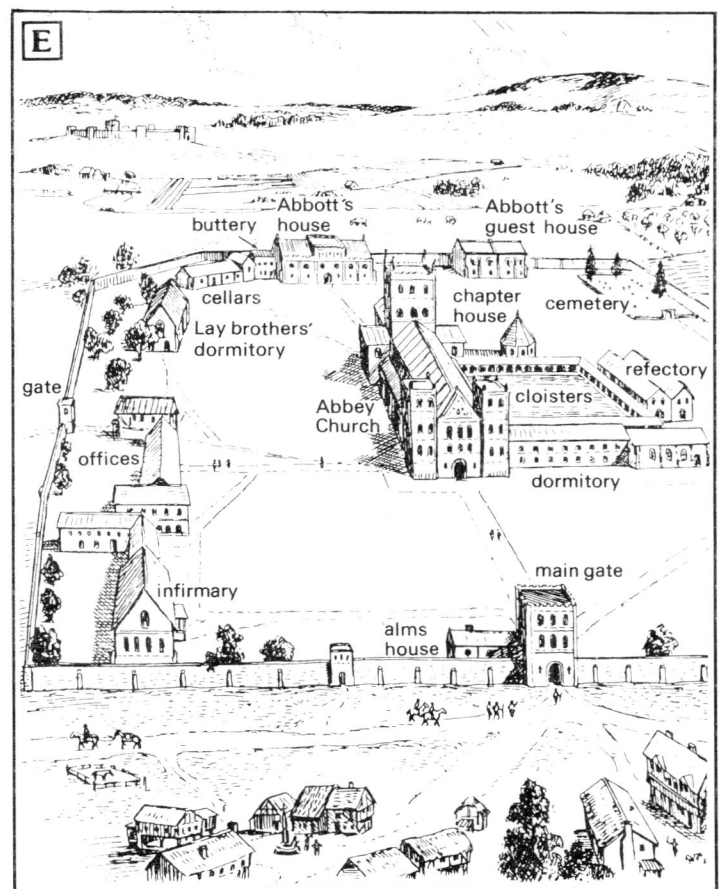

B shows a boy being handed over to monks. Once he was in the monks' care, life became tough.

C *In the bedroom, let the masters sleep between every two boys, and sit between every two boys at other times. When they lie down in bed, let a master always be among them with his rod, and at night with a candle. In the early morning, before the monks wake, the Master of the Boys should rise very quietly and just touch each of the children gently with his rod so that they wake. Then let them rise quickly. If one should hang behind, he is at once to be smartly hit with the rod. This is their only punishment—either to be whipped with the rod or to have their hair yanked hard. They should never be kicked or punched.*

. . . When they sit in the cloisters or in the meeting house (chapter house), let each one have his own tree trunk to sit on. Let them be so far apart that they cannot touch each other. If one of them

sings badly at Vespers because he is sleepy, let the master give him a large, heavy book to hold to wake him up.

Would you still like to become a monk? There were many kinds—*orders*. The rules in **A** and **C** were for boys training to become *Benedictines*. St. Benedict set up the first monastery in the sixth century. He died in 543 AD. **D** is an extract from the rules for Benedict's monks.

Today Benedictine monks still dress as they did in the Middle Ages. If you were a monk, **E** shows the kind of monastery that you might live in. For an idea of how you would spend a day as a monk or a nun, see *The Normans* page 27 **D**.

1 Use the evidence on these pages to say what happened in your first week as a monk or nun. Use these ideas to help you:

Your father brings you to the monastery or nunnery; the service; you dress in monk's/nun's clothes; your daily timetable—lessons, praying, meals, work, sleep; how you get on with the other monks or nuns.

2 List the rules in **D**, saying why each rule was made. Lay out your table like this:

Rule	Reason for it

3 Say how the life of a boy or girl in a medieval monastery or nunnery was different from yours.

SCHOOL AND UNIVERSITY

How would you like to go to the following school?

A *Once I was beaten at school. The class had gone home, and I came sadly to my mother's knee. For, I had been beaten harder than I deserved. As usual she began to ask if I had been whipped on that day. So as not to betray my teacher I denied the fact completely. But, she straight away lifted up my shirt and found the ribs bruised by the blows of the rod, and the skin covered with welts. She was very upset at the heavy cruelty I had suffered, and then stormed and wept, saying, "You shall never be a clerk (a young monk), and you will not put up with punishment to learn your letters." But she promised me that if I wanted to be a knight she would give me arms when I had become old enough.*

The writer of **A** was taught at home, in a monastery or a cathedral. The teacher would have been a monk. The children wrote their lessons on wax tablets using ivory, bone or metal pens. **B** shows a medieval school.

Lessons in monastic or cathedral schools took place in the cloisters or a room of the monastery. The main aim of these schools was to train boys to be monks. They learnt to read the Bible, say mass and sing the chant in the monastery or cathedral. This meant that the boys had to know Latin, the language of the Church. From about 1300 new kinds of schools were set up in many towns, they were called grammar schools. They taught the same kinds of things as monastic schools.

Some cathedral schools had famous teachers, who attracted older pupils who had learnt all that they could in the monastic schools. Sometimes some of the teachers joined together to set up a university, like Oxford and Cambridge (see page 20, map **A**). **C** tells how Cambridge University was founded.

Roger of Wendover (see pages 10-11) tells us:

C *About this time (1209) a certain clerk who was studying in Arts at Oxford killed by chance a certain woman. Finding that she was dead, he fled to safety. But the mayor and many others, coming to the place and finding the dead woman, began to look for the killer in his hostel which he had rented with three other clerks, his friends. And, not finding the guilty man, they took his three fellow clerks and threw them into prison, though they knew nothing of the killing. And, after a few days at the King's command but against all the rights of the church, these clerks were led out of the city and hanged. On this some three thousand clerks, both masters and*

D Age	Subject
7-13	**Monastery School** Reading Chant Writing Mass Learning about God Latin

14-20	**University**
	The Seven Liberal Arts
	Grammar—the rules for
	    reading and writing Latin
	Logic—how to think clearly
	Rhetoric—how to put forward
	    your ideas clearly
	Geometry *Arithmetic*
	Astronomy *Music*

20 +	**Higher Education** Medicine Law Theology

scholars, left Oxford . . . of which scholars some followed their study of the liberal Arts at Cambridge, and others at Reading, leaving Oxford utterly empty.

Students went to university from the age of fourteen onwards. **D** gives an idea of what they learned, and **E** what they read. An account of a poor scholar who went to Oxford and Paris universities tells us:

F *He so much loved learning, that he did not care for food or clothing. As he used to say, he and two friends who lived in the same room had only their tunics and one gown (which they had to wear to lessons) between them, and each had a wretched bed. When one,*

therefore, went out with the gown to hear a lecture, the others sat in their room. Bread, with a little wine and soup was all they ate.

Other students ate, drank, were merry and rioted. The rules of King's College Cambridge said its students should not:

G *. . . keep dogs, hunting or fishing nets, ferrets, falcons or hawks, nor shall they practise hunting or fishing. Nor in any way shall they have or hold any ape, bear, fox, stag, hind, fawn or badger. And it is our will to prohibit games of dice, hazard, ball . . . we forbid dancing or wrestling. . .*

?????????????

1 Draw *or* describe scene **B**. Mark on your drawing or say what the people in the picture are doing.

2 Compare a day in the life of the writer of **A** with your last day at school. Compare:
how people are punished; your classrooms; schoolrooms; your teachers; the lessons you learn; the kinds of things your mother asks you about school.

3 Write a story saying how Cambridge University was set up, as if you were one of the scholars who left Oxford in 1209. Mention:
a the row over the killing of the woman, and how the students were hanged;
b the decision to leave;
c arrival in Cambridge;
d the drawing up of rules for the University;
e the different things that the University taught;
f the life of a good and a bad student.

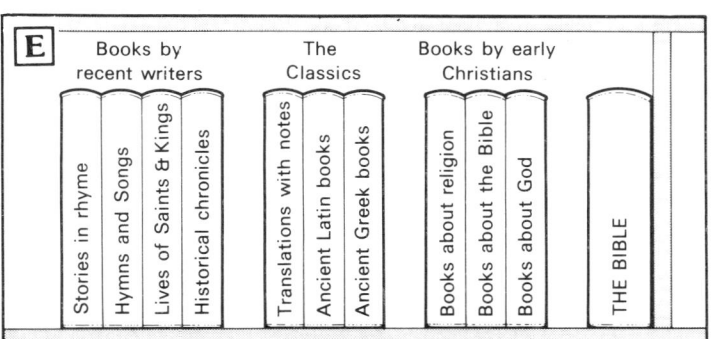

E	Books by recent writers				The Classics			Books by early Christians			
	Stories in rhyme	Hymns and Songs	Lives of Saints & Kings	Historical chronicles	Translations with notes	Ancient Latin books	Ancient Greek books	Books about religion	Books about the Bible	Books about God	THE BIBLE

MONK, NUN, FRIAR AND PRIEST

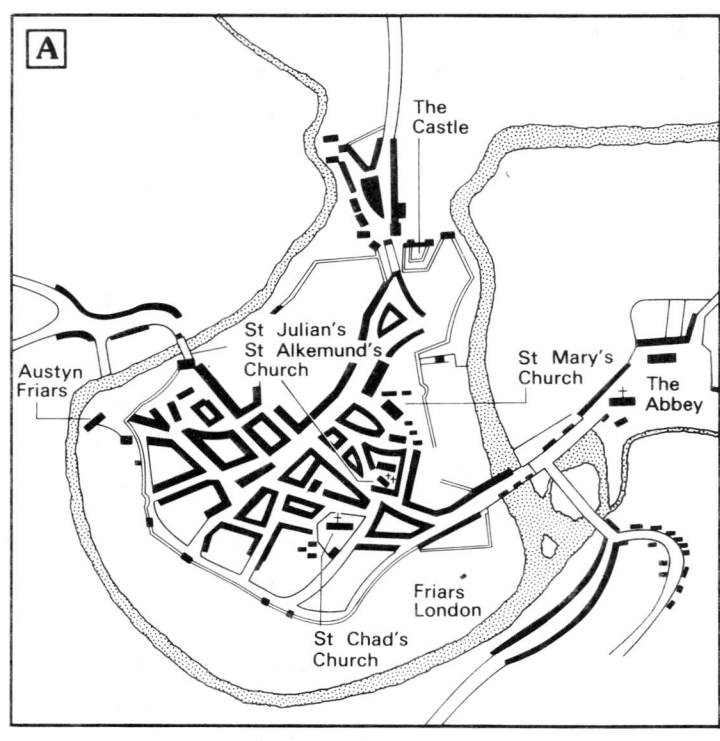

There were many different kinds (or *orders*) of monks and nuns. Most of them obeyed the rules of St Benedict, slightly changed. Many English monasteries were based on the monastery of Citeaux in France. These monks were called Cistercians. Later St Francis and St Dominic founded orders of friars—monks who travelled around the country, instead of in a monastery. The Franciscans wore grey-brown cloaks, and were called Grey Friars. As the Dominicans wore black, what do you think they were known as? A third order of friars were the Augustinians—Austin Friars.

There were also local priests called parsons based on the parish churches. They were like your vicar or catholic father. The map of Shrewsbury, **A**, shows the different churches and religious houses in a medieval town. Parishes were grouped together in a diocese. A bishop was in charge of each diocese. England had two chief bishops, *archbishops*—of Canterbury and York. **B** is a map of the country's main monasteries and cathedrals. A cathedral was a diocese's main church.

A nun, a *prioress* (**C**), went on Chaucer's pilgrimage to Canterbury. A prioress was in charge of a nunnery and did the same type of job as an abbot (see pages 56-57). Chaucer wrote in *The Canterbury Tales* (see pages 54-55):

D *She flashed a smile both simple and most coy,*
Her greatest oath was only "By St Loy!"
And she was known as Madam Eglantyne.
Most well she sang a service, with a fine
Intoning through her nose, as was most seemly.

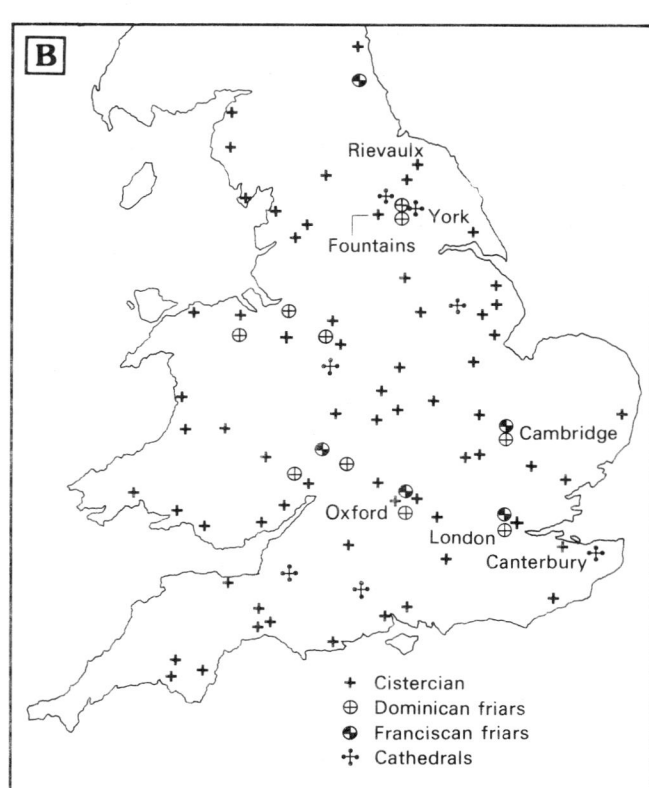

The most important monasteries and cathedrals established by 1300

60

C

She spoke her French most daintily, I spy,
As if she'd learned it at Stratford-atte-Bowe.
French in the Paris style she did not know.
At meals her manners were most well taught;
No bit of grub from her fair lips did sport,
Nor dipped her fingers in the sauce too deep;
But she could raise a tit-bit up and keep
The smallest drop from falling on her breast. . .
Her heart of tender kindness was her boast;
She used to weep if she but saw a mouse
Caught in a trap, if it were dead or bleeding.
And she had little dogs she would be feeding
With roasted flesh, or milk, or fine white bread,
And bitterly she wept if one were dead. . .
Her veil was draped in a most lovely way
Her nose was finely shaped, her eyes glass grey:
Her mouth was small, but soft and dewy red. . .
Her golden brooch hung down both bright and
                                                       gay,
On it was carved a crown above an A,
While below, amor vincit omnia. (Love
                                        conquers all).

Among the pilgrims was a monk.

E A monk there was, one of the finest sort
Who rode the country; hunting was his sport. . .
The rules of good St Benedict (see pages 56-57)
Were old and harsh—so from his mind were
                                                       flicked.
That book he thought not worth a plucked hen
That said that hunters were not holy men,
And that a monk that from his cloisters strays
Is like a fish on land that flaps away. . .

The final holy man on the pilgrimage
was a parson.

F A holy-minded man whose good was known
There was, and poor, the parson of a town.
Yet he was rich in holy work and thought;
He also was a learned man who taught.
Truly he knew Christ's gospel and it preached
Within his parish, and to all it reached.
Most kind, the hours he worked were long and
                                                       hard;
Patient he was when Satan played his card;
He proved his goodness in adversity.
He'd hate to write out the tithe or holy fee.
Indeed, he much liked beyond any doubt
To give to poor parishioners all about
From his own goods and gifts at Easter tide;
For those with wants he'd put it all aside.
His parish was wide, its houses were far away,
Yet failed he not when heavens rains did cry
To pay his call to those in sickness or grief;
The farthest off, whether they be great or small
He'd see on foot—and on them happily call.
This noble example to his flock he gave
To heed God's word so that he would you save.

? ? ? ? ? ? ? ? ? ? ?

1 Which of the rules of St Benedict (see pages 56-57) did the prioress and monk break?

2 Where would these three people stay, if they visited Shrewsbury in 1300, and what would they say about those who lived there:

   an abbot; an Augustinian Friar; a parish priest?

3 What does map **B** tell you about religion in 1300?

4 In your own words, say what Chaucer thought about each of these three:

   the prioress, the monk, the parson.

5 Use the evidence on these pages, and on pages 54-57, to write your own history of the English church after 1100.

EUROPE AND THE WIDER WORLD: MARCO POLO

To pass the time, a prisoner told his cell-mate amazing tales. As he talked, the cell-mate wrote them down. The prisoner was Marco Polo, a merchant from Venice. In 1271 he went to China, and his stories to his fellow-prisoner tell us of his adventures. We learn how people lived, worked, prayed, ruled and fought. Marco talked about everything he saw, even strange animals. At one place he came across:

A *huge serpents, ten metres long and over a metre wide across their body. At*

the front, near their head they have two short legs which have three claws, like those of a tiger. Their eyes are larger than a cream bun, and very bright. Their jaws are wide enough to swallow a man. They have huge sharp teeth. They look so fierce that neither man nor any kind of animal can go near them without being terrified. Others are smaller, being eight, six or five metres long. . . . In the daytime to avoid great heat they hide in caves. From there at night they travel to find their food. They eat any animal they can grab—whether tiger, wolf or any

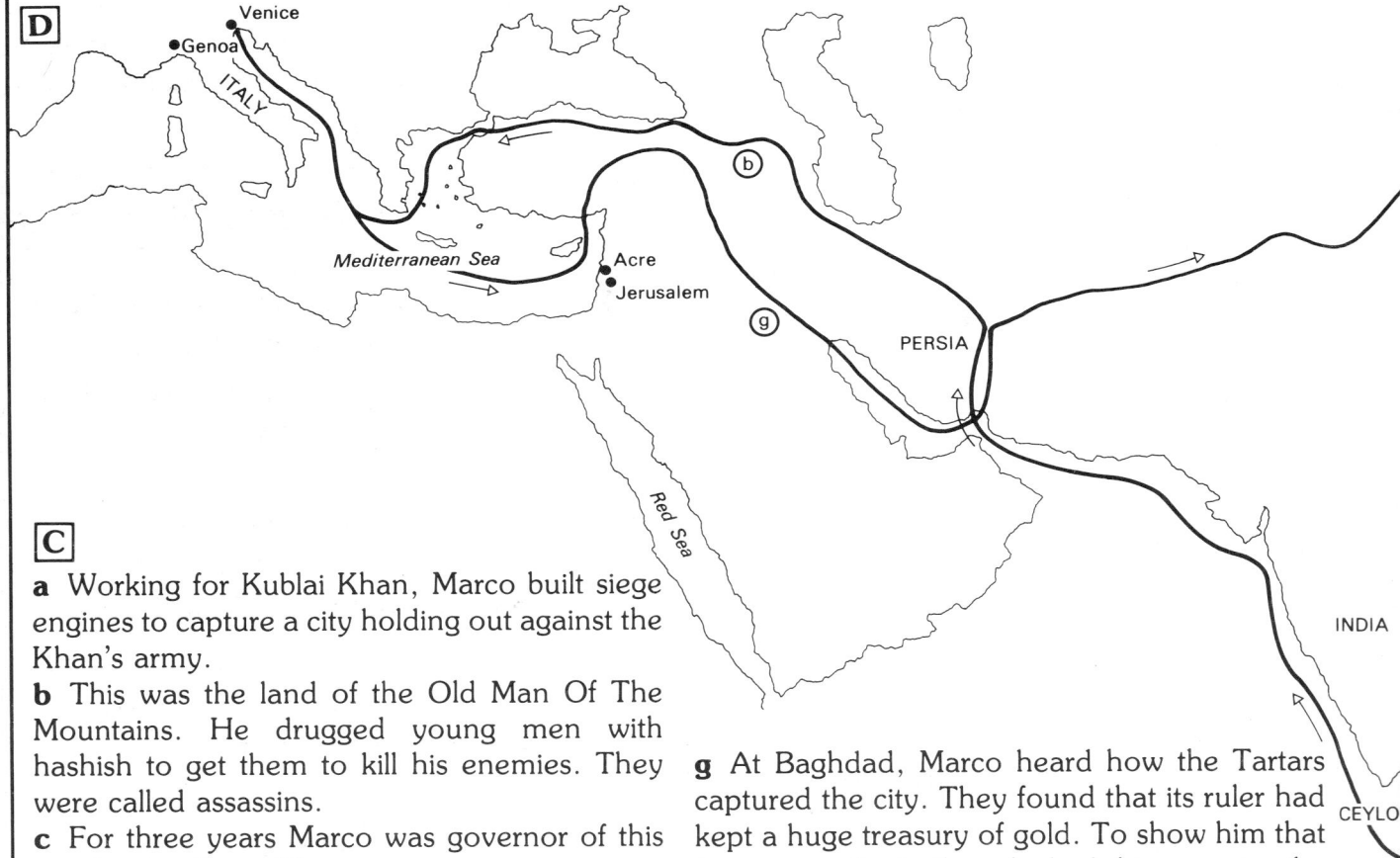

C

a Working for Kublai Khan, Marco built siege engines to capture a city holding out against the Khan's army.

b This was the land of the Old Man Of The Mountains. He drugged young men with hashish to get them to kill his enemies. They were called assassins.

c For three years Marco was governor of this city for the Great Khan.

d Here Marco saw the animals described in **A**.

e Here Marco saw the animals described in **B**.

f Marco used the world's largest bridge to cross a river. The bridge was 250 metres long and had 24 arches.

g At Baghdad, Marco heard how the Tartars captured the city. They found that its ruler had kept a huge treasury of gold. To show him that he was a fool, they locked him up in the treasury without food. There he died of hunger.

h Marco arrives at the summer palace of the Great Khan. For seventeen years he worked for the Khan, and went on errands throughout his empire.

other. After this they drag themselves towards some lake, spring or river in order to drink. Because of their great weight as they move along the shore, they make a deep mark as if a heavy log had been dragged along the sands.

Those who hunt them find the track they use most often and stick into the ground several pieces of wood with sharp iron spikes on them. They cover them with sand to hide them. When the animals go towards where they usually drink, the spikes stab them and they quickly die. Crows begin to caw as soon as they see the dead serpents. This is a signal for the hunters.

Marco sailed to many of the islands of modern Asia. In Sumatra he saw another strange animal:

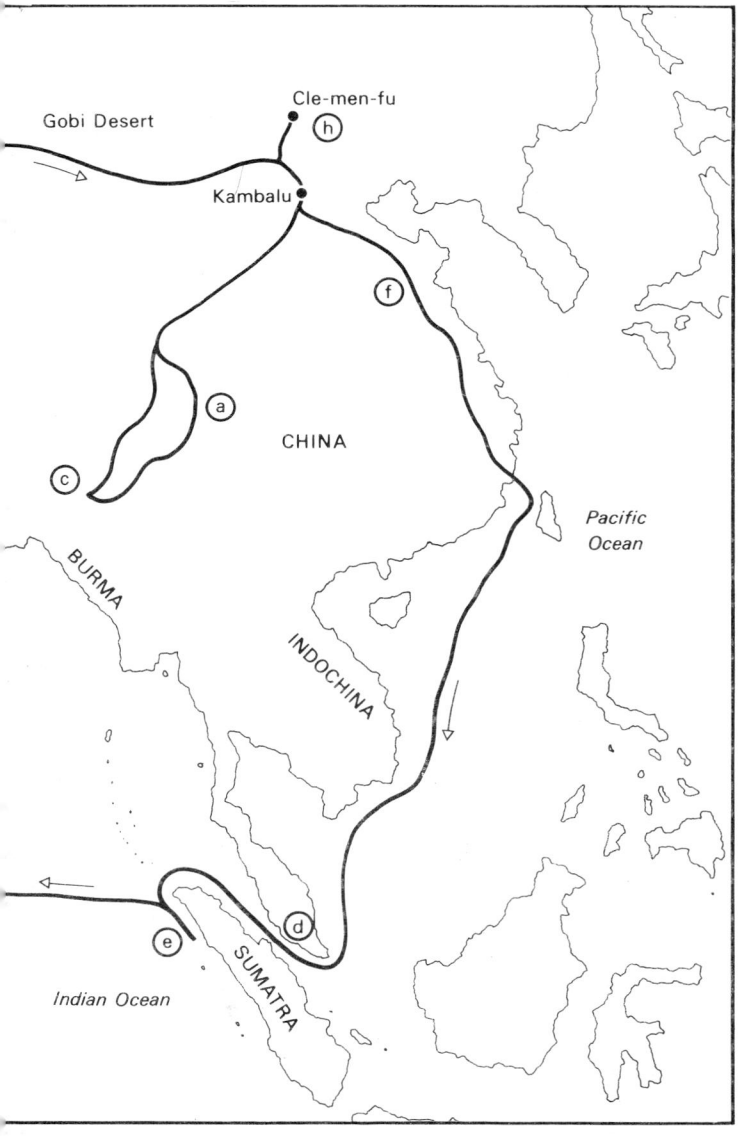

B *smaller than an elephant, but with similar feet. Its hide is like that of a water buffalo. In the middle of its forehead it has a single horn. With this weapon it does not hurt those it attacks. For this purpose it uses its tongue, which is armed with sharp spines, and its feet and knees. Its method is to trample upon a man and then cut him up with his tongue. Its head is like that of a wild boar. It carries it close to the ground. They love to live in muddy pools.*

Marco Polo lived and worked at the court of the Chinese Emperor, Kublai Khan. In 1295 Marco returned to Venice. After this no Europeans were allowed to visit China. For 300 years Marco's book was the only account of Kublai Khan and his lands.

C is a list of things Marco did, saw or heard of. The list is *not* in the order in which they happened. You can work out the order from map **D**.

? ? ? ? ? ? ? ? ? ? ? ?

1 Use Marco's stories **A** and **B** to draw pictures of the two animals.

2 a What animals did Marco Polo describe in **A** and **B**?
b What parts of his descriptions of the animals are untrue?
c What suggests that he had not seen the animal in **B** kill a man?

3 Write a story about a wild animal you have seen on your holidays or travels. Make your story like one of Marco Polo's.

4 Often in newspapers you read stories about travellers. Write a newspaper story about Marco Polo's travels and adventures, in the order in which they happened. Use map **D** and other evidence on these pages.

EUROPE AND THE MIDDLE EAST

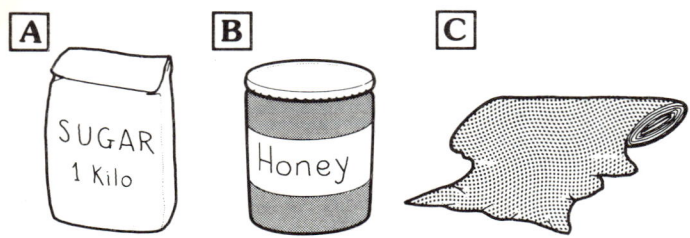

A SUGAR 1 Kilo **B** Honey **C**

The people of Europe learnt many things about the Middle East from the Crusades. What do you put into your tea or coffee to sweeten it—**A** or **B**? Before the Crusades, Europeans did not know about this plant. Why did they like the new sweetener more than the old?

As the Crusaders began to live alongside the Arabs, they copied their dress. At first they wore woollen clothes. Why did they find these uncomfortable? Soon they were wearing clothes made of **C**.

Another thing we learnt from the Arabs was how to count in modern numbers. **D** shows a sum done in both Arab and Roman numerals. Why did Arab numerals become common?

D

XIII	13
+ CVI	+ 106
CXIX	119

The Arabs knew more about science than people in the West. In the Middle Ages, chemistry was called *alchemy*—an Arab word. Alchemists tried to turn other metals, like lead and tin, into gold.

The Arabs were also much more skilled doctors. An Arab doctor told a story about a sick Crusader.

They took me to see a knight who had a boil on his leg. I applied a hot poultice to the leg and the boil began to heal. Then up turned a crusading doctor. He said, "This man has no idea how to cure these people." He turned to the knight and said, "Would you prefer to live with one leg, or die with two?" When the knight said he would prefer to live with one leg, he (the doctor) sent for a strong man and a sharp axe. They arrived, and I stood by to watch. The doctor propped up the leg on a block of wood and said to the man, "Strike a mighty blow, and cut cleanly." And there, in front of my eyes, the man struck the knight one blow after another, for the first had not done its work. Blood poured from the leg. Straight away the patient died.

? ? ? ? ? ? ? ? ? ? ? ?

1 Make a table like this one below to show what Europeans learned from the Middle East. In the left hand column, put what they knew before the crusades; in the right hand column, afterwards.

	Before	**After**
Food Dress Science Maths Medicine Warfare		

2 What is

XIV
− III
?

What is 42 + 94 in Roman numerals?